when GOD winks
on
NEW BEGINNINGS

When GOD Winks on New Beginnings
Copyright © 2009 by SQuire Rushnell

Published in Nashville, Tennessee, by Thomas Nelson®. Thomas Nelson®
is a registered trademark of Thomas Nelson, Inc.

Thomas Nelson, Inc. titles may be purchased in bulk for educational,
business, fund-raising, or sales promotional use. For information,
please e-mail SpecialMarkets@ThomasNelson.com.

Project Editor: Lisa Stilwell
Designed by Scott Lee {scottleedesigns.com}

ISBN-10: 1-4041-8696-4
ISBN-13: 978-1-4041-8696-5

Printed and bound in China

www.thomasnelson.com

09 10 11 12 [WAI] 6 5 4 3 2 1

when GOD winks
on
NEW BEGINNINGS

Signposts of Encouragement for
Fresh Starts and Second Chances

SQUIRE RUSHNELL

THOMAS NELSON
Since 1798

NASHVILLE   DALLAS   MEXICO CITY   RIO DE JANEIRO   BEIJING

TABLE OF CONTENTS

INTRODUCTION

New beginnings are exciting!

But…they are also scary.

Uncertain thoughts creep into your mind.

- *Will this new chapter in my life be everything I hoped for… or a disaster?*
- *Am I really qualified to take on this job…or will they find out I'm quaking in my boots?*
- *Do I really have what it takes to complete this quest— the time, the energy, the stamina? Or will people end up making fun of me…calling me a "dreamer"—and making it sound like a bad word?*

The loudest voice you hear at times like these may be your own, screaming, "WHAT IF I FAIL?!"

If That Happens to You...

Then please go right back to the top of this page and hold on to those first four words: **New beginnings are exciting!** They become exciting to us because they offer the promise of hope, the anticipation of change in our

Change your thoughts and you change your world.
Norman Vincent Peale

lives, and the prospect that our dreams will indeed come true!

As you come along with me in this book, I invite you to infuse yourself with optimism, to ride on the adrenaline of possibilities—and not to plummet on the fear of impossibilities. I'll be urging you to set your gaze upon your desired outcome, to see yourself victorious, to enjoy what you seek—and not waste time on the what-ifs of failure.

Incredible Godwink Stories

I'm betting that the following life-altering stories about people just like you, who have stood on the threshold of new beginnings, will help embolden your perspective and attitude. That's because these stories are about people who simply sharpened their resolve while others belittled their dreams and prognosticated negative outcomes. They simply pulled a cloak of perseverance over themselves, climbed onto their life's highways, and headed for what they believed to be their destinies.

You will see how each of these people was guided by signposts of encouragement: the "Wow, what are the odds of that?" experiences when someone out of the blue "just happened" to intersect their path, steering them into a whole new direction or perspective. You'll witness the incredible so-called coincidences or auspiciously answered prayers that helped them navigate the valleys of their journey and joyfully emerge at long-desired destinations with their quests fulfilled.

These remarkable signposts of reassurance are what I call "godwinks." They are the uplifting little messages that happen to every one of us. They are just as meaningful as that wink you got as a youngster from Dad or Grandma. The kind that meant, "Hey, kid! I'm thinking of you right now. Hang in there."

That's a godwink.

This Is About You

Although I assert that the stories in these pages will boost your optimism and outlook, make no mistake. This book is not about the people in those stories. **It's about YOU**. It's about you and your opportunity to do things you never thought you could do. It's about your concerns. It's about turning uncertainties into certainty. It's about your voyage and your victorious outcome.

Let Your Journey Begin

In Lewis Carroll's classic *Alice in Wonderland*, Alice encounters a grinning Cheshire Cat.

"Would you tell m,e please, which way I ought to go from here?" [asked Alice.]

"That depends a good deal on where you want to get to," said the Cat.

"I don't much care where" said Alice.

"Then it doesn't matter much which way you go," said the Cat.[1]

Lewis Carroll's point: "If you don't know where you're going, any road will take you there."

Are you striking out on your own for the first time? Are you a young graduate seeking your first job, buying your first home, or getting married? Might you be at a crossroads of new beginnings—perhaps an empty nester finding your new reason for being? Or someone who's dissatisfied with, or even dislocated from, your current job? In any case, you are standing on the threshold of uncertainty … a whole new chapter in your life.

Therefore, **the very first thing you must determine is where you want to go.**

As challenging as it may be for you to arrive at the answer, the objective is quite simple. And it's similar to the age-old question you heard as a kid: "What do you want to be when you grow up?" It's important to determine what pursuit will best use talents you already have, what will develop interests you've long nurtured, and what will bring you prosperity, happiness, and fulfillment in the process.

To further illustrate my point, imagine my handing you the keys to a car. You slide in behind the wheel. Now

I say to you, "Go and keep going, day in and day out, year in and year out. Just keep going."

You might look at me as if I were totally daft!

You'd probably shout, "Why would I commence a journey without a map and with absolutely no idea where I'm heading?"

Get the point?

You—yourself, not someone else—need to determine **where** you want to go and **what** you want to do in your life. And once you make that decision, you can begin mapping a plan to get there and focusing on that objective every single day.

Look inside yourself, at the goals and dreams God has planted inside you, and identify what you need to be happy, then put things in motion to secure that happiness.

Robin McGraw
From My Heart to Yours

Chapter

1

WHICH ROAD TO TAKE?

When I'm experiencing a fresh start in my own life, when I'm sorting through the options of what's needed to reach my desired destination, my first step is always this: pray. It may sound like a simple exercise, but I've found that when I ask God for enlightenment about which route to take or what preparations I need to make, He always provides signs—godwinks—along the way, reassuring me that I'm on course.

Mindful that my ultimate purpose is to serve Him, I also ask for the divine placement of people and circumstances along my journey to help me get where I'm going.

Surely we all encounter hurdles and pass through valleys of disappointment. Each of us will be tested— whether with financial challenges, medical emergencies, closed doors, or family issues. I know of no one who isn't! But I can honestly tell you this: God has never let me down. Through faith and the patience He gave me, I have reached just about every destination I've set out for.

So can you.

Many of the most successful people I've met or read about had inklings about where they wanted to go in life at an early age, and a lingering desire burned in their hearts even until long after they had reached their goals. Tiger Woods, one of the world's top golfers, wanted to play golf starting at the age of five. By the age of ten, my wonderful wife Louise DuArt, one of the world's top comedic impressionists, saw herself as a star on stage. Howard Jonas, founder of the large long-distance company IDT Communications, was a preteen entrepreneur. Cheryl McKay was also one of those early determiners. In kindergarten, no less ...

Cheryl: Signs of Destiny

At the age of five, Cheryl demonstrated a love for writing.

By the time she was a teenager, Cheryl paid special

attention to the actors' dialogue in every film and TV program she saw. One particular *ABC Afterschool Special* so impressed her that she figured out how to get in touch with the writer/director, a woman named Susan Rohrer.

"How do I do what you do?" Cheryl boldly asked.

"Go to a place like Regent," Rohrer replied, explaining that she was currently employed by a production company housed on the campus of Regent University.

But soon after, Cheryl's laser-sharp focus on writing was suspended by another interest she wanted to explore—acting. Both fields seemed exciting to her, and she needed to figure out which road to take. She and a future actress-of-note Ali Hillis performed in The Children's Theatre, an ensemble company in their hometown of Charlotte, and wowed audiences with a singing duet. After that, Ali was encouraged to pursue acting as a career, while Cheryl—dismissed from a subsequent theater program—received a different message.

"Getting kicked out was my confirmation that I was meant to be a writer," concluded Cheryl.

Cheryl went on to graduate from high school at age fifteen, do her undergraduate studies at a trio of colleges in the South, and eventually follow Susan Rohrer's counsel: She went to Regent University's School of Communication and the Arts for graduate study.

"I applied for an internship with Susan. She didn't take me on right away, but when she did, a lifelong mentoring relationship began between us."

Cheryl always wondered about those coincidences that she'd later come to call godwinks. She thought, *Are they* *God's way of communicating with us?*

A significant godwink occurred when, after college, she returned home to Charlotte and raised enough money to shoot one of the scripts she'd written at Regent.

"Most days, I had two crew members on set, including me, and I supervised a fifty-member cast of actors and extras," she says, acknowledging the audacity of her statement. One of her extras was a girl named Kasey Eldridge.

"You should meet my dad, Rick," said Kasey. "He produces movies and kids' specials."

Little did Cheryl know then how prophetic Kasey's statement was.

After finishing her shoot, Cheryl went on to save up enough money to follow her dream—to go to Los Angeles and begin a career as a screenwriter. It was then that her godwink was finally fulfilled.

"I had just arrived in L.A. when I got a call from Rick Eldridge's Charlotte-based production company The Film Foundry."

They had a writing opportunity for the audio series *Wild & Wacky Totally True Bible Stories* that they were producing for publisher Thomas Nelson, and they wanted her for the job!

"I had taken a leap of faith to go to Los Angeles, and everything fell into place," she says with amazement. "I found an apartment and got a writing job in my first week."

Remaining in Los Angeles, Cheryl worked with Eldridge's company off and on over the next few years when another opportunity emerged. Eldridge acquired the rights to a book by Jim Stovall called *The Ultimate Gift*.

During one of their conversations, Eldridge asked Cheryl if she, among other writers up for consideration, would like to pitch for the project.

She did. And she thought she did well by keeping the heart and soul in the script and suggesting a love interest for the principal actor.

But Eldridge ultimately chose another writer. Cheryl was disappointed, but she also began to understand that all career pursuits are going to produce a certain number of rejections. And when they happen, it's simply time to reposition your attitude and your actions, be glad for the lessons you've learned, and keep moving forward with enthusiasm.

Nine months later Cheryl was suddenly called home to Charlotte. Her dad required immediate heart surgery. As her concern mounted, Cheryl e-mailed everyone in her address book asking them to pray for him.

Not only did God see her dad through heart surgery, but Cheryl learned that her prayer request had produced an additional blessing: One person on her e-mail list was producer Rick Eldridge.

It was an auspicious time. Eldridge was reconsidering his script options for *The Ultimate Gift.* By divine alignment, Cheryl's e-mail arrived just in time to jog his memory of her heartfelt approach to the drama. It also made him aware that, at that very moment, Cheryl was right there in Charlotte. He called to see if she could come in for a meeting.

Skipping on air, Cheryl returned to Los Angeles as a screenwriter.

Eldridge had given her the chance to write her first produced movie, which also meant she had earned a coveted pass to membership in the Writers Guild of America.

One night, halfway through writing the film, Cheryl awoke from an odd dream.

"I dreamed that the movie starred my childhood friend Ali Hillis. That puzzled me."

Cheryl wrote down the dream, which was her habit, suspecting that God uses dreams as one of many means to communicate with us.

Exactly one year after Cheryl got the nod to write the movie, she was invited to the set for the filming. And as a sweet outcome, the feature was being shot not in Boston, as portrayed in the book, but in Charlotte.

Can you imagine the thrill? Cheryl's very first movie, filmed in her own hometown?!

To top this off, she arrived on the set to find a director's chair bearing her name, placed next to other chairs with such famous names as James Garner, Brian Dennehey, and Abigail Breslin.

"Who did you cast for Alexia?" Cheryl asked Rick, revealing her favoritism for the mother of a critically ill child, a character not found in the original book but one she had created for the screenplay. Rick replied by saying they had hired a terrific actress who had starred in the film *Must Love Dogs* and who was the runner-up for the lead in *Beauty and the Beast* on Broadway. Her name was Ali Hillis.

The statement took her breath away! What a major godwink!

If Cheryl McKay ever received a heavenly confirmation that she was on the right track with her destined purpose in life, that was it.

The two old friends welcomed each other and rekindled the friendship that had started years before during their performances at The Children's Theater of Charlotte.

Hugging each other on the set, Cheryl underscored the obvious. "I had to go to Hollywood to make it in Charlotte," she said with self-deprecating humor.

It's fair to say that if Cheryl McKay had not started her life with a road map marked by signposts revealing the true passions of her heart—if she had not been absorbed with writing starting in childhood—she would not be where she is today. She'd be where most people are who have no idea where they want to go … after driving around in circles, they're sitting right where they started.

If you are facing a crossroads and feeling uncertain of your journey—it doesn't matter whether you're in high school or commencing retirement—know that it is *never* too late to begin mapping the course to your dreams. Today … right now … is the time to start charting a concrete path of pursuit.

So … let me ask you. What *do* you want to be when you grow up?

Assessing What You Were Born With

Some of you were born into homes of comfort and affluence. People might look at you and say, "Boy, were you lucky! You didn't have to struggle like the rest of us."

But this latter group may actually feel sorry for you. After all, if you've never known *want*, if your parents gave you everything you needed—food, clothing, medical attention, schooling, and nearly every toy you wanted—you may have a *disadvantage*. You only need to study the number of highly successful people who have risen from backgrounds of difficulty to clearly see that it was their *struggles* that made them stronger.

Many of you will identify with a kid named Tommy Harken who had a hard time in school and an even harder time in life. But, if you're like me, you'll be flabbergasted by what he made of it….

Tom: Yes, Someone's Watching

The first time I heard of Tom Harken was when he

stepped up to a microphone at an awards banquet I was attending in Washington, D.C. It was the annual Horatio Alger Awards that recognizes ten Americans who have lifted themselves up by their underprivileged bootstraps and pressed on to a place of honor and achievement in our society.

Many of the other recipients were familiar names: Henry Kissinger, the former Secretary of State; Wayne Huizenga, the founder of Blockbuster Video; Maya Angelou, the wonderful poet. But the name Tom Harken … that was brand-new to me. Little did I know, it was a name I would not forget.

"I can't believe I'm here," said Tom, his eyes apprehensively panning a room of one thousand luminaries ready to hang onto every word. "I'm just a guy who peddles tacos."[1]

Everyone laughed.

Moments later, these same people would be struggling with golf-ball-sized lumps in their throats and eyes that became uncontrollably misty.

Even as a kid, blond towheaded Tommy Harken had an engaging smile, and his handshake was like a young man's.

"Before I was six, I was welcome in the kitchen of every house on the block and knew every kid and canine in the neighborhood," he recalls.

But a confident exterior can hide a soft interior. It hurt when others called him "stupid."

"I was painfully aware of being slower than the rest of my class."

Unlike kids today who learn numbers and letters on *Sesame Street*, Tom didn't have that advantage. His folks didn't have a TV, which was in its infancy when he was young. Besides, he was a kid long before those kinds of educational programs had even started.

"Learning disabilities were virtually unheard of in those days. Children were considered smart or dumb," says Tom, "and I had a tendency to gaze out the window while the other kids learned their ABCs."

Other than shooting baskets, what he did best was talking to people … like the customers in his dad's tiny grocery store. That, and getting into mischief. If he could have only figured out how to get graded on monkey business, he'd have had straight As.

Tommy, his older brother, and his two younger sisters grew up in a simple house on a small lake in Michigan; the town was called Lakeview and his street could have been the set for *Leave It to Beaver*, the homey TV series. His mom and dad were similar to those quintessential TV parents too. They loved each other and weren't afraid to display it. And they taught Tommy and his siblings that God was always watching over them and that when they pray, God hears them.

But when he was only eight, Tommy's budding faith was about to be severely tested. His life was about to go into a tailspin… .

He was feeling tired. At first, his folks thought he might be dreaming up a way to get out of going to school. But, when his breathing became labored, the doctor sadly recognized the signs of an epidemic sweeping the country at the time: It was the terrible disease called *polio* that killed or paralyzed children.

Doctors couldn't tell if the disease was contagious … how it started … or how to get over it. The only solution was isolation. At a hospital seventy miles from home.

"They tried every treatment you could think of," says Tom, "but I kept getting worse, and people in the isolation ward were dying left and right. I was struggling to just take a breath, so they put me into an iron lung—big tank that looks like something out of an old science fiction movie. I lay there on my back with just my head sticking out, while mechanical bellows forced oxygen into my lungs."

He was captive in the iron lung for months. With only a small mirror reflecting his own little face to keep him company, he was consumed by thoughts that he was about to die.

There were nurses who occasionally entered the room wearing masks, but he could tell they really didn't want to be there. Fearful they might catch what he had, they weren't likely to stop and chat. They would just come in, officiously look him over, and leave.

Is God really watching over me? Tom wondered again and again. *Why would God want to do this to a little kid?*

He prayed anyway, the prayers of a lonely child: "Please, God, just get me out of here. I'll be good from now on. I promise to do what my parents tell me to do."

One night Tommy got sick. He threw up. Lying on his back, he struggled, but couldn't get his hands out of the iron lung to wipe his face. He was afraid to call a nurse, certain that he was a bother to them. So he just lay there, all night, in his own vomit.

The next morning the doctor was making his rounds. Wearing a surgical mask, a white cap, and a long white coat, he bent over Tommy. His eyes filled with concern.

"Tommy, what happened to you?"

"I'm sorry. I didn't mean to do it," stammered Tommy.

"You didn't do anything wrong, son. My goodness, didn't anyone come to help you?"

"I didn't want to bother anyone."

The doctor pulled off his mask and, as best he could, used it as a towel to wipe Tommy's face.

He pulled Tommy from the iron lung, then sat with him on the floor, just holding him tightly, deeply pained that the nursing staff had neglected this child.

Into Tommy's ear he whispered, "Tommy, I want you to know that God loves you. Even when you wonder about

God, He's there, He's watching over you, He's protecting you. Keep your faith, Tommy. Keep your faith."

As the doctor rocked slowly, Tommy felt safe. It was a comfort that he had not felt for a long time. The hugs of that caring doctor prompted feelings that he carried inside him from that day forward.

And that experience, as terrible as it was at the time, was a godwink—a clear answer to a little boy's prayers— and a few days later Tommy's breathing became better. His hope was beginning to rise. Before he knew it, he was in the backseat of the car as his mom and dad took him home.

It was an indescribable thrill. For years, when thinking back on that day, he could still relive the joy he felt while driving home, the joy of watching the treetops, the houses, the people they passed along the way. He was out of prison at last. Out of isolation.

At least, that's what he thought.

Two days later, God tested Tom's faith again.

The doctor visited the house, conducted some tests, and called Tommy's father at the store. He asked him to please come home; he had something important to discuss with both parents.

Glumly, the doctor revealed his awful findings.

"Tommy has tuberculosis," he said. "He must be quarantined. TB is highly contagious. No one can see him."

Tommy's parents were dumbfounded.

Looking at Tommy's mother, the doctor continued, "You'll have to leave his food, change of clothes, and sheets, outside his room. No one can enter, or that person will get sick too."

For Tommy it was an unimaginable sentence.

"It became an ordeal, almost as unbearable as the time I had had to spend in the hospital," says Tom. "I simply moved from the iron lung into a larger cell. I had a big old radio to help me pass the time, but looking out the window at other kids riding their bikes and playing ball was like watching a weird movie with no sound."

One winter day Tom knew that everyone was out of the house, so he sneaked from his room like a prisoner who had broken out. Stealthily he looked around. Then, through the kitchen window, he watched as his dad skated on the frozen lake with other kids from town.

"I could feel the pain of not being with them," remembers Tom.

Of course he could reason that his dad had the right to recreation and enjoyment. Still, Tom resented it. Terribly.

Going back into his room—his cell—Tommy again asked God, *Why? Why? Why?*

God remained silent.

But a few mornings later, Tommy's angry feelings about his dad vanished in a blink of time. He looked out of his bedroom window. There was newly fallen snow. His dad had gotten up early and, by stomping in the snow, left Tommy a message.

It said, "I LOVE YOU, TOMMY."

Because it was the last snow of the winter, Tommy could see those words etched in the snow-covered side lawn until the spring thaw.

Weeks turned into months. Months into seasons. Tommy lost track of time.

Then one day, the doctor, listening to Tommy's chest with a stethoscope, brightened and exclaimed, "Your lungs are clear, Tommy! The congestion is gone!"

After years of being sick, Tommy would once again be able to hang out with other kids, play ball, shoot baskets, and ride his bike 'til sunset. And once again he'd be going back to school just like everyone else.

But, in all the excitement over his recovery, no one calculated the consequences of Tommy's long isolation. The world he had looked at from his lonely bedroom window had passed him by. All his former classmates were taller, smarter, and in seventh grade. Tommy had totally missed the time when other kids learned how to read and write. He was painfully out of sync with everyone.

On his first day back to school, an unthinking teacher singled him out and said, as a bad joke, "Come on up here, Tommy, and show us what you learned while you were goofing off."

As Tommy stood frozen in front of his classmates, his cheeks began to flush.

"I'll make it easy for you," continued the teacher. "Spell *cat*."

The chalk Tommy was holding tightly snapped in his hands. So did his resolve. He left the classroom and never returned.

Tommy's parents tried to reassure him.

"Everything's going to be all right," said his mother with her arm around his shoulder.

"She didn't believe it, and neither did I," says Tom. "But my dad took me aside, and I'll never forget what he said to me."

"Tommy, so far you've had a rotten deal in life. But sooner or later you're going to make it. You're a good worker, and you're going to have to work harder than other people. So remember this: God has a plan for you, and He knows what He's doing."

> "I know the plans I have for you," declares the LORD … "plans to give you hope and a future."
> **Jeremiah 29:11**

With that, Tommy's father offered him a full-time job at the grocery store.

And work hard he did.

Tommy began to develop an extraordinary memory

that augmented his winning personality. Customers loved dealing with him. He would take their grocery orders over the telephone and not forget a single item. No one ever knew that he couldn't read or write.

And as Tommy became a young man, he realized that his father, on that day of the inspiring talk, was also foretelling one of the most important gifts in his son's life. His father had said, "One day you've got to marry a smart woman."

Tom left the grocery store job and used his personality to sell vacuum cleaners. Along the way, he encountered the love of his life: Melba. They fell for each other right away, but Tom, always being a bit slower, was reticent to take the big step, to ask the big question. In fact, he was scared to death. They dated for many months, and she finally gave him an ultimatum. That did it. He popped the question.

Years later Tom was asked, "How did Melba discover that you couldn't read or write?"

"When I made her fill out the marriage license," he said.

No one else found out. It became their secret.

"Melba was the only one who knew me for what I was, and she somehow loved me anyway," says Tom, adding, "God only knows why."

It wasn't always easy for her.

After Tom rushed Melba to the hospital for the birth of their first child, he panicked when the nurse handed him a clipboard and asked him to fill out the forms.

"I couldn't do it. They were going to find out that I couldn't read or write. I'd be a laughingstock," he remembers with anguish.

 So he ran. He left Melba at the hospital on her own. To have their baby boy. He ran back to hide in his work. And, ashamed of himself, to cry alone.

Still, Melba was his best supporter. His biggest encourager.

They became a team. Tom would sell vacuum cleaners door-to-door and memorize all the necessary customer information. Then, when he got home, Melba would fill out the orders and send them in.

Eventually, when RVs were just coming into vogue, they leveraged their teamwork into selling campers. Tom's hard work and winning personality and Melba's good sense and smarts led them to open RV dealerships across the whole Southwest.

Later on, they opened the first of thirteen Mexican restaurants they owned in Texas and Louisiana.

All during those years Melba would quietly encourage Tom to learn to read and write. Because he had always been good with numbers, he could figure out figures. And he learned to read and write enough one-syllable words to get by. But his fear of failure caused him to rely on quick wit and deft sidestepping. Amazingly, he was able to keep his secret from everyone but Melba.

When the kids climbed onto his lap and asked him to read them a book, Melba would quickly swoop in and say, "I'll do it. Daddy's too tired."

In restaurants he'd hand the menu back to the waitress, say, "I've read it before," and simply order a hamburger.

In business deals he'd pass a contract to someone else and say, "I forgot my glasses."

Even when Tom's two boys were grown and had families of their own, they never knew that their father hadn't been able to read while they were growing up. Then, one day, they were asked to go to the family's office building and take a seat in the boardroom.

Sitting across from them and supported by Melba, Tom made the confession.

He told his sons that a wonderful thing was about to happen. That much to his surprise, he had been selected to be one of ten recipients of the 1992 Horatio Alger Awards at a big banquet in Washington, D.C. He wanted them to be there—and, because Melba had convinced Tom that it was time to tell the whole story, to finally fess up that he'd been illiterate most of his life—he wanted them to know it first.

Tearfully, as his sons stared at him in shock, Tom asked for their forgiveness for all those years he had curtly replied, "Go ask your mother," when they had asked for help with their homework.

He further explained that their mother, little by little, over the years, had helped him finally learn to read and write.

And now, Tom said, he was going to share the secret of his shame in a banquet room filled with important people.

Many times, in retrospect, I've pondered my own godwink of that evening—the divine alignment that brought me to that event on that particular night in Washington. It had been a last-minute invitation from friends to attend and sit at an open seat at their table. When Tom Harken stepped up to the microphone, I was as engrossed as everyone else. With a trace of uneasiness in his voice, he said, "This is the first time I have ever read a speech to an audience like this."

As Tom took us on the epic journey from a boyhood spent in an iron lung, to the epiphany when a doctor gave him hope and assured him that God had a purpose for him, to the man who struggled throughout life trying to hide the shame of his illiteracy, to that very moment of receiving Horatio Alger Award—he confirmed what is written in the ancient Scriptures: "In all things God works for the good of those who love him" (Romans 8:28).

Henry Kissinger later said to Tom, "Out of the thousands of speeches I've heard in my lifetime—speeches by presidents and kings—I remember only about five. Yours is one of the five I will remember."

A few months later Tom's picture was on the cover of *Parade*, a magazine read by eighty million people. A career of public speaking soon blossomed. Tom became an encourager for untold thousands of people who also harbor the secret of illiteracy.

Tom's story bolsters the faith of all those who wonder, "Does God really hear us?"

Ask Tom.

The answer is yes.

 The Course of Action

Both Cheryl McKay and Tom Harken drew upon the desires and talents they displayed in their early childhood to determine where they wanted to go later in life. Cheryl found her love of writing by the age of five, and Tom discovered his winning personality and amazing ability to talk to people when he was about ten years old. Their early attributes shaped the paths each determined they would travel.

Cheryl studied hard—graduated from high school at fifteen, attended four colleges, and earned a master's degree. Tom's path was quite the opposite. Failing to learn how to read and write until adulthood, he relied upon his good-natured personality, his work ethic, and his life experiences in order to achieve some extraordinary goals. These individuals had two completely different approaches to life, yet both exemplify the merits of mapping what course you intend to follow in life, and to reach for specific goals that you set for yourself.

"It is never too late to be what you might have been."
George Eliot

Chapter

2

THE EMPOWERMENT OF BELIEF

Cheryl and Tom shared another value that is paramount to every person striving to reaching one's objectives: **they believed in themselves.**

And that was possible **because they believed in God's promises for them.**

Where are those promises found? In an ancient book of wisdom that is over three thousand years old. The Bible.

- "I will not break my covenant; I will not take back one word of what I said" (Psalm 89:34 TLB).

- "You know with all your heart and soul that not one of all the good promises the LORD your God gave you has failed. Every promise has been fulfilled; not one has failed" (Joshua 23:14 NIV).

You're on His GPS

It's comforting to know that we're always on an incredible GPS—God's Positioning System.

Not only is God watching your back at all times, but you have the privilege of a personal relationship with Him. He invites it. He wants you to talk to Him daily; He wants you to talk to Him as often as you like. He appreciates it when you thank Him for the favor He's given you, and you can absolutely *expect* that He will answer your requests of today—often communicating back to you through godwinks of reassurance.

I think you'll agree that every relationship is enhanced by constant communication. This is true of your relationship with your parents, spouse, siblings, or friends. You've no doubt learned that, over time, ongoing communication with colleagues at work develops mutual respect and harmony.

It is therefore not surprising that frequent communication between you and your Maker will also result in a stronger relationship between the two of you. The more you communicate with Him through prayer, the more you'll notice a strengthening in your faith. And the stronger your faith in Him grows, the more faith you will have in yourself.

Do Prayers Really Work?

People who put their trust in God—who make it a practice to ask for His blessings and who truly expect to receive them—will attest, over and over, that prayers really work.

In our lives, Louise's and mine, prayer is a proven power every single day. For that reason we initiated a movement to get couples to pray five minutes a day for forty days, The 40 Day Prayer Challenge. In almost every case, couples report back with enthusiasm that it has been a life-changing experience.

Baylor University/Gallup research that we uncovered for our book *Couples Who Pray* suggests that when two people pray together regularly, there is a 20 to 30 percent increase in romance, conversation, and happiness.

We also cited Duke University studies attesting to the power of prayer in health issues and longevity. Dr. Harold

Harold Koenig, the university's associate professor of medicine and psychiatry, reported that "Senior citizens who said they rarely or never prayed suffered significantly more health problems than those who prayed with some frequency."[1]

Prayer and Godwinks

In my definition of a godwink, I contend that it encompasses answered prayer.

god•wink (god´wingk)w

*A personal signal or message directly from God,
sometimes as an answer to prayer,
and often mislabeled as coincidence.*

Watch the role prayer played in the following story, producing an extraordinary, life-saving godwink.

Franklin: God Winks Darkness into Light

Nightfall descended over Jackson, Mississippi, and Sydney McCall, tower operator at the small local airport, was wrapping things up for the day. His last radio communication was with the pilot of a Texas-bound plane that was leaving the Mobile area, south of Jackson's airspace. Sydney acknowledged the pilot's location and passed him on to air controllers in Shreveport.

Outside the tower, the airport slipped into darkness as Sydney's efforts to close down for the night were interrupted by a fellow worker.

"You expecting guests?"

He returned a puzzled look, which faded as soon as he remembered a conversation he'd had that morning in church with Forest Hill Baptist's Music Director Gary Cornett. During coffee hour, he had invited Gary to come by and see how an airport operates.[2]

"Come on over after closing, and I'll show you around the tower," Sydney had said proudly.

He smiled as Gary and his wife, Pat, were ushered into the control tower.

Meanwhile, the small plane that Sydney thought had gone on to Shreveport was actually in deep trouble.

At the controls of the Texas-bound plane was an unseasoned pilot, college student Franklin Graham, who was flying back home after a weekend visit with his parents in Vero Beach, Florida.[3] Next to him was flight instructor Calvin Booth, who had been invited along to ease Franklin's parents' anxiety about him making the journey alone. Calvin's wife, Dorothy, and a friend, Lee Dorn, occupied the backseat.

Minutes after Franklin had left the Mobile area and had his last radio contact with the Jackson air controller, the instrument panel lights began to flicker slightly. Franklin turned up the rheostat to make them brighter. Yet, during the next twenty or thirty minutes they dimmed more and more as Franklin followed his charted course, which skirted the Gulf of Mexico in order to avoid heavy thunderstorms predicted for the area.

The flags on the instrument panel suddenly flipped to the "off" position. The cockpit quickly darkened to pitch-black, and the radio went dead.

"I've just lost my navigational instruments," Franklin said to Calvin with measured calmness.

Both men groped for their flashlights and began to plot a course of action. They were above heavy cloud cover and didn't know exactly where they were.

"We were forty miles south of Jackson when you talked to that last tower," said Calvin, looking at the charts in his hands. "We were at about twelve thousand feet. We need to get down to about fifteen hundred feet and see if we've gotten to the Jackson area," he added, masking a growing fear.

Furrowing his brows, Franklin eased the turbo-powered Cherokee Comanche down through the dark, heavy clouds. As he broke through the layers, a faint glow of city lights emerged from below.

"That's probably Jackson," said Calvin.

Franklin glanced to the backseat. Dorothy and Lee were fervently praying. Gripping the flashlight in his teeth, Franklin continued his descent. Two thousand feet … fifteen hundred feet … the city lights were brighter, clearer. But where was the airport? Was it closed?

Back in the control tower, Sydney picked up a tricolored light gun and held it for his visitors to see.

"This is how we can communicate with a pilot who has lost radio contact," said Sydney. "We have a red light … a white light … and a green light."

Turning from his visitors, Sydney held the light gun toward the window and shined it into the black sky.

"If I wanted to give a pilot clearance to land, I'd turn the green light on and point it directly at the plane."

Gary and Pat nodded.

Placing the light gun on the console and moving his hand to a silver knob, Gary continued his explanation. "This switch here is for the airport runway lights," he said pointedly. "The runway lights are geared to operate at different levels. This is normal intensity. If we put the lights at the *highest* intensity"—and he turned the knob to that level— "it would be for emergencies. In this position, the lights are designed to pierce the cloud cover to help pilots find the runway."

Wide-eyed, Gary and Pat looked out the tower windows. What had been total darkness moments before was now a burst of brightly lighted runway. As Sydney continued his talk, Gary and Pat nodded, then watched the runway fade to black as he turned the lights off again.

In the cockpit of the Cherokee Comanche, Franklin spotted a green light piercing the clouds.

"Look! The tower has seen us!" he shouted gleefully. "A green light! We've been cleared to land!"

Cheers arose from the backseat where Dorothy and Lee lifted their heads from prayer.

"You'll need to lower the landing gear manually," said Calvin, hurriedly. "There's a handle between the seats under the floorboard."

As Franklin lowered the landing gear, Calvin took over the controls and descended in the direction toward where they had seen the green light.

Then, right on cue, an airport runway burst into illumination. The runway lights on highest intensity meant the air traffic controllers had spotted them and were welcoming them in for a landing!

Calvin guided the small plane down with a precise, smooth landing.

More cheers of joy erupted from everyone in the plane.

Then,… oddly … no sooner had the wheels touched

down … the lights went out. The airport was totally dark.

"Hey! That's strange. They could have at least waited until we got off the runway before shutting down the lights," said Calvin, with a trace of annoyance.

Back in the control tower, Gary Cornett was extending his hand to Sydney.

"We sure appreciate your taking the time to give us a tour," he said. But his comment was interrupted by an excited airport worker shouting to Sydney.

"An unlighted plane just landed!"

"What?" exclaimed Sydney, with an astonished look on his face.

A short while later, four relieved and immensely grateful passengers entered the small airport, making introductions all around. And during that moment of ecstasy, completely unknown to everyone, two parents in Vero Beach—famed evangelist Billy Graham and his wife, Ruth—were continuing to fiercely pray for their son's safe return to college in Texas.

Dr. and Mrs. Graham had no idea their conversations with God that night would produce such extraordinary lifesaving godwinks for their son: that with precise, supernatural timing, a green light would be aimed directly at Franklin's troubled aircraft, pierce through the night clouds, and signal him to a safe landing just as a runway miraculously radiated up out of the darkness. It was as though the light of Jesus arrived in the nick of time and led Franklin to a safe landing in answer to their prayers.[4]

Godwinks and Perfect Timing

Sometimes godwinks arrive with unbelievable timing and extraordinary flair—the way we'd expect to see God's divine involvement portrayed in a Hollywood movie. But most of the time, godwinks are small messages of reassurance that just "happen" to show up, not at all ostentatiously, at divinely appointed moments, to let us know He's watching over us. In Jeani Stevens's case, the Almighty seems to have a knack for communicating through godwinks and license plates ….

Jeani: Unexpected Signs of the Road

"Over the years there were seasons of frustration, hurt, and unforgiveness," says Jeani Stevens, describing her relationship with her former husband Bob, "but they were dotted with civility, tolerance, and occasional agreement."

During the first four years of their marriage, Jeani and Bob were blessed with two beautiful children. What followed were two decades of attempts to live together in peace.

Then came the doctor's report that crashed into their lives like two cars in a head-on collision: Bob was diagnosed with an incurable disease called amyotrophic lateral sclerosis—ALS for short. Also known as "Lou Gehrig's disease."

The doctor explained that Bob's muscular system would deteriorate to a point of complete paralysis. Labored breathing would lead to an inability to speak or swallow.

Worse, Bob's specific ALS was a type that is genetically transferable. Jeani and Bob's children would be forced to not only watch their father die, but they would remain under a cloud of uncertainty as to if and when they too would develop symptoms of ALS. Jeani's whole world was turned upside down.

"In a moment of time, a person I would have liked to figuratively kill after a painful divorce suddenly became a person I would have done anything for, if it meant saving his life."

What could she do?

Pray.

Jeani found herself with a new quest in life: she prayed for Bob's physical and spiritual healing.

"One day," she said, "I was on my way to church, thinking about him. I wept. I prayed."

Then, in her rearview mirror, Jeani took note of a long white limousine approaching from behind, tailgating her at first, then swinging around and passing her. Initially annoyed, she then spotted the license plate. It read, "ALS 03."

That's odd, she thought.

A decal sign in the rear window of the limo provided a clearer definition. It said, "ALS—Angel Limousine Service."

"Right then and there, I knew God was communicating with me … and that He was working in Bob's life."

Subsequently, the divine alignment of a new job opportunity caused Jeani to move from Northern

California to San Diego where Bob and their two grown children lived.

"I surprised myself, and probably others, when I volunteered to help care for Bob a day or two a week," she said. "It enabled me to demonstrate to our children the importance of forgiveness and helping people who need help."

As Bob's health deteriorated, caring for him became more and more challenging. Rising fuel prices and the one-hour drive to Bob's were also exacting a price.

"God, why am I doing this?" Jeani prayed in anguish one day as she slowed for a traffic light. The license plate on the little red sports car that pulled in right in front of her had the answer: "4 God."

"It was loud and clear. I got the message: I was doing it for God."

When Bob passed away, Jeani wrote of her experiences and lessons in a book called *Benches*. "I sat on life's bench with Bob Dennis for more than half of my life," she wrote. "During that time relationship scars were healed and Bob watered the seeds of Christ's love in my own life. Now a garden grows."

Moreover, Jeani's prayers for her former husband's

spiritual healing were answered.

"Bob diligently sought to find God," she says. "I believe he found Him."

Jeani Stevens finds God by keeping her eyes open for Him. She sees His presence in godwinks every day. Sometimes even on other people's license plates….

While driving home from a business meeting with her friend Penny Brown, Jeani excitedly explained that she had recently been contacted by *The 700 Club* on ABC Family Channel about doing a film piece on her experiences with answered prayer.

Penny, still tentative about the power of asking, believing, and receiving God's blessings, exclaimed, "I wish that would happen to me. What do I have to do to have more God experiences?"

Once again, a car with an auspicious license plate passed Jeani's vehicle. This time it was a PT Cruiser that pulled in front of them.

The license read: "KP PRAYN."

"There's your answer, Penny," squealed Jeani with delight. "Just keep praying!"

Chapter 3

WHERE HOPE COMES FROM

The ancient Scriptures tell us that "faith is the substance of things hoped for, the evidence of things not seen" (Hebrews 11:1 KJV). Let's think about that.

The biggest reason people give for doubting God is that they are unable to "see" evidence of His existence. Yet the centuries-tested wisdom of the Bible says that our faith assures us that the things we hope for are indeed possible, even though we may not yet see them with human eyes, and that they will come into evidence when we continue to trust Him.

Imagine if your "dream in life were to help children, including your own, who are born into this world with severe disadvantages. But as you looked around, you found there was no place that provided the kind of hope they deserve—the hope of becoming self-reliant, hope that would elevate their self-esteem, and hope that would enable them to realize that they have a purpose in life.

If that were your dream in the midst of such a stark reality, how great would your faith be that God would open enough doors and enough wallets to help you fulfill your dream. Listen to Yvonne's story ….

Yvonne: The "Why" Question Answered

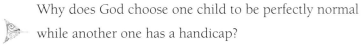

Why does God choose one child to be perfectly normal while another one has a handicap?

That question probably crosses the mind of every parent of a special needs child.

Many of us, including me, do find an answer—though, not right away and not when we expect it. Usually in some unanticipated moment, a light shines through and we come to understand, very deeply, that God has chosen us, for His own special reasons, to parent a developmentally challenged child. And that, in so doing, He has honored us.

As an infant, Vicki suffered from mumps, encephalitis,

and meningitis prior to the natural formation of a protective coating over the cells of her brain. This caused severe head trauma and resulted in extensive brain damage. She spent almost four of her first eight years of life in a hospital.

There were times when Yvonne, her mother, was at her wit's end. She and her husband, Dave, asked every question, pursued every resource, and considered every option in their efforts to find Vicki the very best medical and rehabilitative care.

One of the leaders in the field of rehabilitative special education for the handicapped was Dr. Newell Kephart of Purdue University. Yvonne and Dave heard of his program and made arrangements to take Vicki for an evaluation and attend one of his seminars.

Dr. Kephart asked, "What does Vicki respond to?"

"She responds to almost nothing," said Yvonne in a firm voice. "If you put her down in the middle of the floor, two weeks later she might still be there."

"Everyone responds in some way to something," countered the doctor. "We just have to find the *something* that will initiate a response in Vicki."

But try as he might, in test after test, Vicki provided no response. She demonstrated no signs of recognition. She emitted no sounds…. There was nothing.

The famed Purdue specialist remained determined. He decided one day to conduct his seminar in a gym that was equipped with a trampoline. He carefully laid Vicki on the trampoline and, standing next to it, bounced her up and down. At the break, he said his arm was about to give out, so he switched and bounced her with his other arm for the remainder of the lecture.

 When Dr. Kephart finished his talk and stopped bouncing, Vicki lifted her head slightly and gasped, "Auuuuugh."

Vicki had responded! Articulating dismay that the bouncing had ended, she had uttered her first sound.

It was a joyous moment. But the next several years were tedious for Vicki's parents. Dr. Kephart outlined a program that might help Vicki become more aware of her environment. Every day, for several hours, Yvonne would repeatedly place her hand over Vicki's little hand to teach— with kinesthetic, motor, and tactile input—how to grasp an object, lift it, and release it.

Years later, this hard-earned ability would give Vicki the opportunity to productively hold a job in a horticulture program. And her mother would proudly say, "Last year Vicki grasped, lifted, and released eleven thousand potted plants into flats."

In many ways, Vicki was God's ultimate gift to Yvonne and Dave. This sweet, special child became the catalyst for the development of two outstanding Houston-area institutions. One is a school that has taught over ten thousand learning disabled children, of whom an astonishing 87 percent have gone on to college. In the second case, Vicki was the inspiration for the founding of the exemplary Brookwood Community for adults with functional disabilities, the community that continues to be her place of work and residence.

As Vicki grew toward adulthood, Yvonne began to realize that a facility was needed to provide opportunities for people like Vicki to learn how to contribute to society. Practical education was the key. As the vision formed in her mind, she pictured a loving, God-centered community where its residents could be taught meaningful skills for work and everyday living, skills that would enhance their lives, promote self-esteem, and help provide clarity about God's purpose for them.

As God planted that desire in her heart, Yvonne studied how and where such a facility could be initiated. The more she learned about other residential schools in New England, Chicago, Germany, the Netherlands, and England, the more she realized she needed to do more research. Each of the schools she studied had something good to offer that she hadn't seen anywhere else. She sought to uncover the best practices at each facility and then adapt them for the plan that was emerging in her mind. But, she concluded, more research required funding.

"I gave talks at one Rotary Club luncheon after another, trying to cultivate interest in this vision, but to no avail," she said, chuckling with self-deprecation. "You know, they let *anyone* speak at Rotary."

Again and again she spoke about the monetary support necessary to research the building of a revolutionary place for adults with functional disabilities. "We weren't getting anywhere," says Yvonne with a note of despair. "After almost a year I felt I had totally failed. The only money we'd raised were the small contributions my husband and I had put in. I was ready to throw in the towel."

"Did I hear you wrong, God?" she asked the Almighty.

The very next morning at 8:30, the phone rang. It was Frank McGuire, a man who had heard Yvonne speak at a Rotary luncheon.

"I'd like to give you something," he said.

McGuire arrived at her office at 9:00 a.m. and handed Yvonne a check for $10,000. "To study the idea for Brookwood," he said.

"I was flabbergasted," said Yvonne.

That same morning at 9:30, Yvonne's assistant director gleefully shared more good news: "A man who heard you at Rotary telephoned. He's sending over a check for $7,500!"

At 10:00 a.m., St. Luke's Methodist Church phoned.

"We're sending you a check for $25,000 to study the Brookwood idea," they said.

At 11:30 another call came. This one from The Barrow Foundation.

"We are contributing $30,000 for your study."

All of this occurred within two hours!

"Hallelujah!"

Yvonne and her staff were overjoyed and thanked God for the emphatic "GO!" they had received.

The thing about godwinks is that you never know when to expect them. But when God *does* wink, you'll know it's Him! It may be in the eleventh hour. You may be ready to give up hope. But stay alert. Godwinks are His way of reminding you that you're never alone in the tasks you've been handed or the missions He's led you to choose. Godwinks bear a similar message to that long ago wink from Grandma—"Hey, kid! I'm thinking of you right now. You're not alone."

Today, nearly three decades later, Brookwood Community sits on one corner of over 475 acres in south Texas. It serves as a model for thousands of other institutions. Parents and teachers come from around the world to study why it's so successful in lifting the self-respect and self-reliance of some 110 residents and 50 daytime attendees.

Remarkably, the dedication and hard work of the citizens themselves produces one-third of the income needed to sustain their community. Houston area visitors have learned to telephone well in advance to reserve a table at The Brookwood Café in order to enjoy fine dining under the guidance of a Culinary Institute of America chef and where the wait-staff, consisting of Brookwood residents, check boxes on a specially designed pad to take your order. After lunch, visitors can browse through a gift shop with items that could grace the pages of *Better Homes and Gardens*, displaying the many professional-looking crafts of Brookwood residents. Or they can purchase geraniums and other potted plants from a nursery that stretches the distance of a football field and seems to dare visitors to find a single brown leaf.

"God has His hand on every plant," says Yvonne with a flourish. "The heart and soul on which Brookwood is built is the awareness of what goes on in the minds of our citizens. We show our people how to take pride in their room and their dress, how to be proud of what they can actually do, especially what they didn't *think* they could do.

"At Brookwood, we cajole our people … push 'em … and even bribe 'em to reach a little higher," says Yvonne good-naturedly. Switching to a more serious tone, she adds: "But don't you think for one moment that this has anything to do with me. God caused all of this to happen. Every bit of it. We're doing just what He has led us to do."

Yvonne's favorite godwink experiences seem to underscore that belief. God started it all with Vicki, and Vicki's achievements—by the grace of God—ignited in others the desire to help by forming Brookwood. Then God unfolded a series of incredible godwinks on that single morning with contributions totaling $72,500 dollars.

God is indeed awesome.

Faith is believing in things
where common sense
tells you not to.
George Seaton
Miracle on 34th Street

Chapter

4

STEPPING OUT IN FAITH

My grandmother Mama Alice was fond of a particular quote. She would say, in her British accent, "God helps those who help themselves." For the longest time I thought she was quoting the Bible. Then, when I grew up, I found out she was quoting Benjamin Franklin. Nonetheless, the statement has stuck with me, and, as I have experienced life, I now see the wisdom in it.

God does not expect you to sit on your baggage by the side of the road, waiting for your destiny to be delivered to you. Instead, He expects you to get up, leave your baggage behind, and get on life's highway heading for what you believe to be your destiny in life. And when you do get moving, He will bless you with unbelievable godwinks of reassurance all along the way.

I have two stories that demonstrate that, when you put yourself in motion, when you step out in faith, you'll see the "substance of things hoped for, the evidence of things not seen" (Hebrews 11:1 KJV).

The first story is my own… .

SQuire: Winks in a Green Volkswagen

I grew up in a relatively poor family in a small farming community in northern New York, twenty-five miles from the Canadian border. People were fond of saying it was a "one-horse town," which was almost true. In fact, we had just one of everything—one grocery store, one gas station, one doctor—except we had more than one horse and lots and lots of cows.

As a kid I would listen to my radio at nighttime and before sunrise, when the signal brought in faraway stations, and I'd fantasize about going to those places.

When I was in sixth grade, I got a chance to go to a distant city to visit a radio station. That day changed my life. From the age of eleven on, I had a laser-sharp focus on a career as a radio announcer. Morning, noon, and night I would talk into my sawed-off broom handle, pretending it was a microphone. I was particularly pleased that my imitations of on-air personalities drove my older brother bananas.

I'd come down for breakfast emulating Dean Harris, my favorite faraway disc jockey, by echoing his overly enthusiastic command, "Get up and march around the breakfast table!"

A cereal box might whiz past my head from the direction of my annoyed older brother, Win.

When I was fifteen, I somehow landed a job interview with Jim Higgins, the head of the only radio/TV complex in our county. It was ten miles up the road in Watertown, New York, and my only means of transportation seemed relatively safe at that time—hitchhiking.

However, a country road can mean a long wait in between vehicles. A few hay balers went by. A few pickups. And very few cars.

I began to worry that I might be late for my very important appointment.

Just as I was starting to get discouraged, a little green

Volkswagen pulled to the side of the road. The door burst open, and a large balding man beckoned me in. I told him where I was going and the purpose of my mission: I had my first job interview with the man who ran the radio and television stations in Watertown.

When I came up for air, the man stuck out his hand and said, "You tell Jim Higgins I said hello."

I looked at him in astonishment.

"By the way, my name is Dean Harris."

My mouth dropped open and spread to a grin!

Can you imagine that? Getting picked up on a country road, driven to my very first job interview, in the business that became my career, by my hero—Mr. March-around-the-Breakfast-Table Dean Harris!

Now, *that's* a godwink!

Oh yes. I got the job—my first job in the business that was my life for the next four decades.

As I look back on that day in my hometown of Adams Center, New York, I realize that I could never have gotten to those distant, faraway places I heard about on the radio if I had not listened to the desires of my heart … if I had not dreamed big dreams … or if I had not "helped myself" as Mama Alice had taught me, stepping out and heading in the direction I believed my destiny was taking me. In my case, I *literally* stepped to the side of the road, and hitchhiked my way on to my life's highway.

And, if I had not been talkative, if I had not told Dean Harris where I was going and who I was meeting, he may not even have identified himself.

Like me, Debbie Supnik has found through personal experiences that highly significant godwinks have occurred when she has stepped out, taken initiative, and carried on conversations with others ….

Debbie: The Fabergé Egg Hunt

"What are we going to do?" asked Debbie in a voice swelling with anxiety. "We've looked everywhere. We're no closer to solving this puzzle than we were two months ago."

Debbie Supnik, a diligent television producer and head of development for Weller/Grossman, a Hollywood-based production company, spent eight weeks attempting to get a lead … any lead … on identifying and locating an heir to the fabled Fabergé family.

Her company had successfully pitched A&E Television a one-hour documentary for the network's *Biography* series on the history of the famed Russian jeweler Peter Carl Fabergé, who created the priceless egg-shaped art treasures. To tell the story—and not lose the production order—they had to locate an heir to Peter Carl Fabergé, who rose to prominence in the late 1800s when the Empress of Russia

spotted his elaborate jewelry designs at a Moscow fair. The Empress told her husband, Czar Alexander III, about the young jeweler's decorative art skills.

Czar Alexander then secretly sought out Peter Carl Fabergé and commissioned him to design a decorative egg-shaped piece of art for his wife as an Easter gift. So extraordinary was Faberge's creation that he and his heirs were given an imperial appointment to create a new egg-shaped art treasure every Easter for the next fifty-four years.

To give you an idea of the value of Fabergé's decorative art today, one of his creations sold at auction in 2007 for $18,000,000.

Utterly frustrated, Debbie was getting nowhere in her efforts to locate any of the heirs to the original Fabergé family. She learned that The House of Fabergé was entirely different from the American perfume company that had acquired the name. Moreover, decades of turmoil caused by the Bolshevik Revolution and World War I had scattered the Fabergé family across Europe, and, in the pre-Internet time of this story, finding anyone who knew the whereabouts of any heirs was just about impossible.

Debbie was frankly relieved and ready to take a break when her husband, Paul, asked her to join him on a trip to England with their eleven-year-old daughter Kate. Paul was a member of an international association of lawyers that was meeting in London.

For five days Debbie and Kate busied themselves in various shopping and sightseeing activities that helped Debbie temporarily forget the disappointments of her quest to find a Fabergé heir.

On their final day, they were in the Piccadilly area, and Kate was drawn to the Burlington Arcade, a cozy street with small shops selling items like sweaters and ascots.

"Are you sure you don't want to get back to the hotel?" Debbie asked plaintively.

She was tired. She'd walked the Burlington Arcade many times in the past, so it held no charm for her.

"Let's go in here," said Kate brightly. It was a clothing accessory shop, and Kate found something she wanted to purchase for an uncle.

They stood in the shop and talked between themselves as they waited for an older man in front of them to complete his purchase.

The dapperly dressed gentleman, with ascot and walking cane, turned.

"You're American!" he said with enthusiasm.

"Yes, we are," said Kate very proudly.

For the next few moments, they chatted amicably.

Moving on, the man then held out his hand and introduced himself.

"I'm Theo Fabergé," he said. "It was nice to meet you."

Debbie was aghast.

"Are you related to the House of Fabergé?"

The man nodded.

"I ... I ... I've been looking for you," she stammered, quickly explaining her quest to find a Fabergé heir.

"You found one," said the gentleman, brightly. "And I'll be happy to help you." He handed Debbie a business card that she quickly placed into her handbag for safekeeping until she got back to Los Angeles.

Thanks to this extraordinary godwink, Debbie was able to save the *Biography* production and deliver to A&E Television one of its most popular programs. As evidence of success, for the next three years the biography of Peter Carl Fabergé, told by Theo Fabergé's great-granddaughter Tatiana Fabergé, was among the network's best-selling videos.

Yet ... the godwink would never have happened if Debbie and Kate had not engaged a pleasant gentleman in conversation. Their talking to a stranger in a small, obscure shop in a foreign country led them to a destination, and that path was marked by an incredible godwink.

Chapter

5

HOW TO REPURPOSE REJECTION

Gordon Morton, head of marketing for a health beverage company called XanGo, once said, "Every kid who works the counter at McDonald's has heard the word *no*. When placing your order, they'll ask, 'Do you want fries with your meal?' and when you say no, do they go into a corner and put their thumb in their mouth? Of course not. They say, 'Next!'"

Gordon's comment supports my own notion: The word *no* is one of the smallest words in the dictionary. Its relevance should therefore be minimized.

Sometimes *no* means "No, not right now," which may signal that you can revisit the matter later.

Other times *no* is a clear, unmistakable closed door, in which case you can be grateful for a straightforward, honest response. You were not left in a state of uncertainty, so you can move on like the kid at McDonald's.

In any case, receiving a *no* is never a time to wallow in hurt feelings.

It's Not about You

When someone refuses a suggestion or idea we have, our first inclination is to take it personally, concluding that we are being rejected. But that's not the case.

Zig Ziglar, an outstanding sales coach, recalls his own early years as a salesman. He said, "I had a serious self-image problem. I took the word *no* as a personal rejection. That meant I would have to spend time alternating between pouting, meditating, having a pity party, and planning what to do next. How I wish someone had explained to me that when people turned down my marvelous offer, they were not rejecting me. In their minds it was a simple business refusal. The prospects really had no interest in the offer itself and would have said no to anyone."[1]

Let's think about this thing called *rejection*. The fear of rejection is really the fear of getting our feelings hurt, isn't it? And that fear of rejection can cause us to react in all sorts of ways, like procrastinate and make up all kinds of excuses why we shouldn't begin a project or pick up the phone to make that sales call. We start letting our imagination become our reality. We say things like, "Well, it's Monday. Therefore so-and-so will just be getting back from the weekend and have a lot of calls piled up, so there's no point in calling today."

Or we'll rationalize why someone hasn't returned our phone call by making up imaginary answers like, "She knew (somehow) what I was going to say and isn't interested." Then we'll willingly accept an imagined turndown and not bother to call back at all! Now, really, how silly is *that*?

When a busy person has not responded to a letter or presentation I've sent, I recall my own days as a buyer of network TV programming. Scores of videos and submissions would land on my desk each week. Often a person whose presentation was in the pile would follow up with a phone call. I would usually avoid the call because I hadn't yet made the time to look at his or her proposal.

Imagine that you were one of those people who sent me a pitch letter. Every day you stared at your mailbox awaiting a reply. You began to wonder, *When in the world is he going to return my call? Does he hate my idea so much that he can't bear to tell me?* You started to feel anxious and concluded that I didn't like your idea. But in reality my lack of response had nothing to do with your idea at all. The problem was on my end: I was dealing with my own issues of lack of time and organization. (I'm referencing when I was a thoughtless, disorganized network executive.)

Still, thinking back, I remember what prompted me to finally fish someone's videotape out of the pile and reread the letter. It was when my secretary would say, "Mr. So-and-so asked if it is okay for him to call back on Friday morning to see if you've had a chance to view his tape." Frequently that impetus was all that I needed to correct my own organizational deficiencies, pull his presentation from the pile, look at it, and be ready for his call on Friday.

We have to dismiss those negative suggestions that creep into in our imagination. We have to stop putting words into the mouths of people we haven't spoken to. We have to refuse to accept negative thoughts about our ideas that haven't even been considered! We have to look at our fears in the bright light of day, when we can have a clear and proper perspective, and then face them with our eyes wide open.

What follows is a story about someone you may have heard about. Just like you and me, he's faced rejections. There's nothing unique about the rejections; only in how he dealt with them ….

Steve: Repurposing Rejection

At birth, Steve was rejected twice.

First, his mother rejected him by putting him up for adoption.

Second, the adoptive couple awaiting his arrival wanted a girl. So they rejected him too.

Notwithstanding, everything turned out pretty well for Steve. A nice couple finally *did* adopt him, gave him a nice childhood, and, by scrimping together every dime, saved enough to send their son to a small college.[2]

Yet Steve wasn't what you'd call a social kid. Instead, he was the type who liked to figure out how things worked; he would take objects apart and put them back together again—just for the fun of it. What's more, Steve had no idea what he wanted to do in life.

Thus, college wasn't a comfortable fit. He couldn't comprehend why the courses on his required list— history, geography, philosophy—were necessary or how he'd apply what he learned in whatever career he decided to pursue.

So, after six months, he dropped out.

But what about his folks? He couldn't let them down. So Steve remained at college … and dropped *in* on courses that were of interest to him.

For instance, he dropped in on a calligraphy course. For no particular reason, learning about serif and sans serif typefaces and about the artistic subtlety of spaces between letters fascinated him.

But, by year's end, Steve got busted. His parents found

out, and they made him return home.

When he did, Steve hung out with his old buddy, Woz. They started tinkering with a gadget—a computer—in the garage. They called it an Apple.

Ten years later, at the ripe old age of thirty, Steven Jobs and Woz had gone from two guys tinkering in a garage to running a $2 billion company. In his lap, he proudly held his brand new Macintosh computer.

And then … he got fired.

What?! How do you get fired from your own company?

He simply had a run-in with the board of directors, and this time he was rejected big time.

Steve was devastated. He later said he thought he had let down all entrepreneurs. He was about to run away from the Silicon Valley altogether. Then he thought, *Wait … I love what I do. I'm an inventor … I just need to reinvent myself.*

Steven Jobs said later, "I didn't see it then, but it turned out that getting fired from Apple was the best thing that could have ever happened to me."

He repositioned his rejection and started over.

"The heaviness of being successful was replaced by the lightness of being a beginner again, less sure about everything. It freed me to enter one of the most creative periods of my life."

Steve set out to start a company he called NeXT, and its mission was to inaugurate a new technology. And a while later, with the pain of failure and rejection in his rearview mirror, Steve had another brainstorm. *Wouldn't it be great,* he thought, *if we could use computers to generate an entire animated movie?*

So he started a second company called Pixar. He led the development and production of the world's first fully animated movie with CGI—computer-generated imagery. The movie was called *Toy Story.*

As Steven Jobs focused on nurturing the growth of his two new companies, the firm he once founded was floundering. Apple was on the ropes. Wall Street gurus said the once-inventive computer manufacturer was washed up.

The board of directors at Apple determined they

needed something new in order to survive. A new technology. The kind that Steven had developed at NeXT.

What sweet revenge! Apple came back to Jobs with their hats in their hands. They bought NeXT, and once again Steven Jobs was wandering the halls of Apple. That gave him the opportunity to make the board of directors another offer they couldn't refuse: Hire him back as CEO for one dollar a year.

Apple did eventually pay Steve a real salary. And it happened just about the time he and his colleagues at Apple came up with iPod—a technological development that altered how the world listens to music. The success of iPod then led to iPhone, and Apple became a $160 billion company. (Yes, an interjection—like "Wow!"—is appropriate here.)

That's what you can do with rejection: Reinvent yourself.

Steve says, "None of this would have happened if I hadn't been fired."

Where's the Godwink?

You may be asking, *So where's the godwink in this story?*

When Steven Jobs was making his first Macintosh, he asked his engineers, "What if we were to offer, instead of one typeface like the PCs have, a whole array of fonts: serifs, sans serifs, and so on?"

That's right. The godwink of why all computers today have multiple fonts started when Steven Jobs dropped *in* on that calligraphy course years before.

The next story is not just about rejection, but about incredible perseverance, which is exactly what you must have when you face multiple turndowns.

Vin: Putting the Ten in Tenacity

Vin DiBona is one of those names that rolls off your lips. You almost want to say it the way you'd expect a waiter in Little Italy to repeat it, complete with customary hand gestures. Vinnnn Di-BON-a!

You'll remember Vin's name if you've ever seen *America's Funniest Home Videos*. And who hasn't? The show he created is ABC's longest running series with more than eighteen years on the air. And, yes, there was a godwink or two along the way ….

About the time Vin was making a name for himself in Los Angeles as a producer for *Entertainment Tonight*, he was on a trip to Japan.

He spotted a TV series that looked like fun. It was sort of a *Candid Camera* with animals. He learned it was one of the most popular shows on Japanese television and contacted the network to see if he could get a limited option to acquire the funny film footage to take back to America. He imagined he could weave the film clips into a celebrity panel show … sort of like *What's My Line* or *American Idol*. The film clips would be stopped just before their funny endings, and the celebrities would have to guess what was going to happen next.

The Japanese TV executives agreed to give Vin the clips on one condition: that he also option another of their programs, one that featured home movies. Vin had no idea what he'd do with that, but eager to make the deal, he agreed.

Vin and I worked together at a TV station in Boston when he'd just gotten out of UCLA. We remained friends through the years as we both developed our careers.

While he was making his way as a Hollywood producer, I was running *Good Morning America* and Children's Television. I would often hire him to produce special events and program segments.

Yet, when Vin developed his new program—which he called *Animal Crack-Ups*—he never brought it to me. After all, he perceived his show would be targeted for adult audiences and have no application for my children's programs.

Often this maxim comes as a rude awakening: There are few slam dunks in life. Tasks and opportunities we've imagined as sure things are usually much more difficult to pull off than we anticipate. Although Vin could clearly envision the merits of his programming idea, other network and syndication executives didn't get it. Every meeting he held ended with a turndown.

Over and over Vin made his pitch. He'd reanalyze his presentation. Tweak it again. Then he'd pull way down into a seemingly bottomless reserve of tenacity and continue scheduling meeting after meeting, once again pumping up his enthusiasm and rearticulating his vision for *Animal Crack-Ups*.

His proposal was rejected 136 times.

His option to use the Japanese TV clips in a TV series was about to run out.

He decided, in one last desperate shot, to call his old pal SQuire.

Vin had no way of knowing that back in New York, I was going through one of those struggles that sometimes occurs in corporate life. The legendary Roone Arledge, who was in charge of ABC sports programming, called a meeting with our joint boss. He laid out an argument that my Saturday morning kids' programming, leading into his Saturday afternoon sports block, was delivering audiences of kids. Who knew? He reasoned that if *he* could take over the last half hour of my schedule, at 12:30 on Saturdays, his department would produce a kid-adult program with dual audience appeal.

He made a very persuasive argument. And I didn't like that our mutual boss was nodding a lot.

Dejectedly, I returned to my office thinking, *If I don't come up with my own kid-adult program, I'm going to lose my time period!* Moreover, my fall schedule was due to be announced in just a few days.

The phone rang. It was Vin.

In a short, carefully rehearsed pitch, Vin explained the idea behind *Animal Crack-Ups*.

I could see it. A fun show. Celebrities. The wacky animal footage that could be positioned as educational. It had both kid *and* adult appeal.

"Great! Let's do it," I said.

There was silence on the other end of the phone. Then Vin spoke.

"You want to do a pilot?"

"No. Let's do thirteen half hours."

Boom! That's often how godwinks work in life. They can come bursting in at the last moment, delivering you a direct message from above, that your hard work, patience, persistence, and, most of all, faith are now going to pay off!

I think God delivers His winks that way just to show us that it could *only* have happened through Him.

Vin DiBona's *Animal Crack-Ups* was a great little show. It

did everything I needed it to do for my Saturday morning schedule, and it delivered the necessary adult viewers for Roone Arledge's lineup.

For Vin, it gave him the cachet of being a *network producer* and a lot of inside access at ABC.

A short while later, Vin walked down the hall to "ABC Primetime programming. In a six-minute meeting he pitched them a show using that other Japanese footage—the home videos. He called that show *America's Funniest Home Videos*. The rest is history.

Yes, once in awhile slam dunks *do* happen. And most likely they are extraordinary godwinks of divine alignment!

By the way, you'll be happy to know that I never held it against my friend Vinnie that he placed me last on his list of 137 pitches.

In the final analysis, Vin taught me a powerful lesson. No matter how many times you get turned down…if you believe in your idea…if you believe in yourself…and if you believe in God…you can come out the victor.

Who puts the *ten* in *tenacity*? You do. Never try just once or twice to advance an idea that you know in your heart has merit. Ten attempts might only be the beginning.

> Success is the ability to go from one failure to another with no loss of enthusiasm.
> **Sir Winston Churchill**

"If you do what you fear, you won't fear what you do," says Gordon Morton, "and after a while you realize that rejections are very much a part of life."

When I catch myself procrastinating or making little excuses—sure signs that, truthfully, I am avoiding something I am actually fearful of doing—I think of something my wife once told me. As a professional comedienne performing under her maiden name, Louise DuArt, she started out in life painfully shy. Yet she launched her career the only way possible—by getting up to the microphone at comedy clubs. In her mind, she has always struggled to keep her dream bigger than her fear. And, the very thing she feared—getting up on stage— *invited* rejection.

"Being a stand-up comic is the process of harnessing rejection," she explains. "In order for Jay Leno and Jerry Seinfeld to hone their act, they go on stage somewhere and try out new material. They eliminate the jokes that are rejected by the audience and improve upon those that aren't."

For me, my wife's concept has been a good impetus. I ask myself, *Would I rather make this phone call, or go on stage and be rejected in front of many people?*

I make the call.

Keep your dream bigger than your fear!

Chapter

6

FINDING YOUR COMPASS

O ver a period of four decades, millions of high school and college graduates have launched their career pursuits by studying an immensely popular book with a curious title: *What Color Is Your Parachute?* The advice of author Richard Nelson Bolles is so brilliantly simple and filled with common sense that few other books have ever successfully competed[1] ....

Richard: Opening Your Parachute

A godwink of a lifetime occurred in the late 1960s when Richard Bolles, an Episcopal priest, was working for a San Francisco church that was undergoing a budget crunch. At a meeting Bolles learned that many of his colleagues were reading the handwriting on the wall, so to speak. They were bailing out and starting to look for other jobs.

To underscore that their apprehensions were registering with him as a manager, Bolles picked up a piece of chalk to list their concerns on a blackboard. Yet, at the last instant, instead of writing the words *bailing out*, he whimsically scrawled, "What color is your parachute?" He had no idea that single line would turn out to be one of the most significant godwinks in his life.

"It was just a joke," says Bolles.

It was no laughing matter, however, when he lost his own job a few days later. But Bolles was more fortunate. He promptly landed a job counseling people in need. Feeling compassion for his still-out-of-work colleagues, he determined that they would benefit from a primer of sorts, a guidebook to help them find new employment.

After researching the matter, Bolles wrote a 168-page document with down-to-earth advice. When he was stuck for a title, he remembered what he'd scribbled on the blackboard. He placed that on the cover *What Color Is Your Parachute?*

It turned out that there was such demand for his simple guidelines, that *What Color Is Your Parachute?* was eventually published as a book.

In 1991 the Library of Congress did a survey asking people the top twenty-five books that had shaped their lives. Answers ranged from the Bible to *The Wizard of Oz*. The only business book on the list was *What Color Is Your Parachute?*

Sound Advice That's Just as Relevant Today

In his mega bestseller, Richard Nelson Bolles articulated the worst and the best ways to look for a job.[2] In capsule form, this was his message:

THE FIVE WORST WAYS TO FIND A JOB

1. Job postings on the internet.

   4 to 10% success rate depending on job category

2. Mailing out resumes at random.

   7% success rate

3. Answering ads in trade journals.

   7% success rate

4. Answering newspaper ads.

   5 to 24% success rate depending on salary levels

5. Employment agencies and search firms.

   5 to 28% success rate depending on salary levels

THE FIVE BEST WAYS TO FIND A JOB

1. Asking for job leads from family, friends, or school.

   33% success rate

2. Approaching any employer that interests you, regardless of any known openings.

   47% success rate

3. Using the Yellow Pages in the city you wish to work, then calling or visiting the employers.

   69% success rate

4. Band together with others, in a "job club" to follow the strategy of item #3 above.

   84% success rate

5. Life-Changing job hunts; doing extensive homework on yourself before seeking employment. Determine: WHAT skills you currently have that are transferable; WHERE, like a flower, you are best likely to bloom;

HOW to get where you want to go by creating a list of names of people and organizations.

86% success rate

Richard Nelson Bolles takes you through each of those points in his annually updated book, *What Color Is Your Parachute?* His classic has been considered such a must-read for so many graduates and people at the starting gate of new beginnings that it has sold more than ten million copies.

To me, one of the most significant messages of that book is that we should look to our passions … not to the want ads … to try to identify the occupation of our future. That certainly was the case in Michael's story. He turned a passion into a highly impressive outcome ….

Michael: Seven Encouraging Words

Michael snuck into the basement where his mother maintained a small ceramics workshop. He found a well-used pot and tiptoed back up the stairs to the kitchen where he ignited a burner on the stove. With surreptitious glances at the door and out the kitchen window, he began to melt chunks of canning wax. As it melted, he stripped the paper coverings from several dark red crayons, snapped them in two, and dropped them into the concoction. Then he patiently watched them diminish in size with each turn of the wooden paint stirrer. Streaks of red blended into the clear wax, eventually creating a smooth light reddish color.

To the side he quickly readied his mold—a milk carton cut in half—into which he would pour the melted wax and then insert a wick salvaged from an old broken candle.

At sixteen years of age, Michael had a simple quest: He wanted to make a candle for his mom for Christmas. Though he didn't know it at the time, making this gift was an auspicious step onto his life's path. Three decades later, Michael would sell the company birthed that day in his mother's kitchen for … $500 million. The company was called Yankee Candle.

How could a boy with a desire to be a rock-and-roll guitarist end up becoming one of America's most prominent candle makers? What extraordinary godwinks dotted his path and provided messages of encouragement just when he needed them? And what can *you* learn from Michael's experience that will help propel your career?

"Did you make that for your mother?" asked a woman attending a ceramics class led by Michael's mom.

Michael nodded. He proudly held the candle he'd fashioned on the kitchen stove.

"That's beautiful," she cooed. "May I buy it?"

Surprised, Michael hesitated. But he agreed and sold it. For two dollars.

That meant, of course, that he would have to make another one for his mom for Christmas. So he did—and, fortunately, he kept *on* making candles when he discovered that many people were willing to pay two bucks apiece for his creations. Furthermore, Michael reasoned the timing couldn't have been better: The rock band he'd started four years earlier had entered into a period of dormancy when its oldest member went off to college.

During his remaining two years of high school, Michael escalated the sales of his little candle business that was now encroaching his mother's ceramics space in the basement. He learned how to purchase canning wax in larger quantities in order to make more candles at a time and to lower his expenses, and he discovered that he could choose from a whole variety of candle molds, giving him a wider range of creativity. Each time he revved up the old stove, he improved his technique, his timing, and his style. Pretty soon he emerged with a signature look that he called "Candles by Michael Kittredge."

Michael found several shops willing to sell his candles, yet he continued to enjoy interaction with his regular customers in the neighborhood. He would carefully dissect their reactions and comments to determine what they liked the most about his candles and what they didn't care for. He discovered, for instance, that adding a scent to the candles increased their appeal.

"Will the candle smell like roses when I light it?" asked one woman, holding a rose-scented candle to her nose.

"Unfortunately, no," he told her. But further experimentation led him to an important discovery: If he put five times the fragrance into the mix, the candles would indeed smell like roses … or lilacs … or an apple pie cooking in the oven … when they were lighted.

Adding the extra fragrance created a problem, however. Oil-based fragrances used in heavy doses would not bond well with the wax and cause the candle to "weep." So Michael introduced the idea of putting a candle in a glass jar.

Today, that simple idea is an industry standard.

During his first three years in the candle business, Michael's rock-and-roll pals teased him.

"They thought I was crazy … making candles in my parents' basement. Meanwhile, my mom and dad's friends forecast nothing but a dire outcome for my entrepreneurial career, and my folks were getting tired of my messing up the house."

An exception to the crowd of naysayers was Uncle Kraemer who lived in Florida. Michael met him in person only a few times, but via occasional long-distance telephone calls, Uncle Kraemer was robust with his encouraging statements. Like a lone light on a darkened road, the counsel of his father's brother pierced through just when Michael needed the reassurance. As if divinely appointed.

But that's what happens in life.

We go barreling along thinking we're totally alone. Everybody else would have done things differently, and they tell us so. The droning of discouraging comments weighs us down. Then, out of the blue, someone comes into our path. He calls us on the phone. Or we bump into her. And that person ends up changing the whole direction of our life, whether through a new career, a new love, a geographical change.

I believe these people are Godwink Links—unwitting messengers of assurance who are divinely directed to deliver godwinks to you and me.

Not only that, but you, too, are an unwitting messenger at times. You are sometimes a Godwink Link … delivering godwinks to others … without even knowing it.

These occurrences just prove that we're all on a super GPS—God's Positioning System.

Michael's mini-business finally overwhelmed his mother's ceramic workshop in the basement. It expanded into the garage, it overtook his bedroom, and it even burst the seams of an old tin shed in the backyard. His conglomeration was becoming more than an annoyance.

He also changed the name of his enterprise to the more professional sounding "Yankee Candle."

Since there was only one telephone line into the house, Michael insisted that all members of the family refrain from answering with a mere "Hello!" and instead use the more professional response "This is Yankee Candle."

His mother resisted. "Why do you have to be such a big shot?" she challenged, adding that most of the calls to the house were from her friends and family.

To counter this noncompliance, Michael strung a phone line down the cellar stairs, so that he could race to the ringing phone and answer it with the appropriate professionalism.

The growing popularity of Yankee Candles among gift stores in his Massachusetts hometown of Holyoke escalated sales. Soon his territory expanded to neighboring South Hadley and even ten miles up toward Amherst. To keep up with the demand, Michael worked late into the night squeezing in his studies at Holyoke Community College and later at the University of Massachusetts-Amherst.

One semester Michael was assigned to meet with a career counselor. It was a ten-minute session with a professor he'd never met, presumably designed to help him wrestle with that age-old question, "What in the world am I going to do with the rest of my life?"

Michael provided the professor with a short synopsis of his interests, described his part-time candle making, and explained that, given his druthers, he would love to become a rock-and-roller. Or maybe a teacher.

Dismissing Michael's first desire, the professor focused on some of the foibles of a teaching vocation.

"There are just too many teachers out there," said the man, "and the pay is not very good."

Michael searched the professor's eyes for answers.

Then, offhandedly, the man said, "Why don't you try the candle thing?"

It didn't seem like a godwink at the moment. But those seven words—*Why don't you try the candle thing?*—from an authoritative adult gave Michael, for the first time, permission to do what he had been doing out of pure passion for the past five years. No other person had ever suggested that earning a living by candle making was even a reasonable option.

Michael spotted an ad in a Holyoke newspaper: 2000 square feet for rent in a mill section of town for $88 a month. The task of turning the unheated former chrome-plating plant into a workable space—its walls were layered in a stubborn black substance, and electricity was imported via extension cord from a neighboring shop—was arduous. On winter days the only heat in the building was generated from the candle-melting stoves, and Michael learned the hard way that leaving unfinished candles overnight only caused them to freeze. Sixteen-hour days were therefore the norm.

During the first two years Michael worked in the old factory, his sales to gift shops doubled each year.

One day two women found their way past the

corrugated tin door, peeked inside, and asked if Yankee Candles were sold there.

Michael invited them in and showed them around. Before leaving, they bought $80 worth.

Within hours Michael put up shelves, lined them with candles, and placed a sign outside. The first Yankee Candle retail shop was officially established. Soon, newspapers found the story interesting—a young candle maker was growing a business in Holyoke's mill section— and his shop began to flourish.

Every year sales expanded by 25 to 30 percent or more.

In his fourteenth year, Michael reached an important benchmark for any entrepreneur: He had $1 million in annual sales.

It was time to expand his business exponentially. To do that, he needed to vacate the old industrial city of Holyoke. After all, it had grown into disrepair when so many mills elected to move south.

In 1983 he relocated to a perfect piece of property visible from and in between two exits of a major highway in Deerfield, Massachusetts. It was a bold move. He bought as much land as he could, and that was fifteen acres.

The first official Yankee Candle store provided parking for six cars, but within hours of opening, that proved insufficient.

A while later, in the mid-1980s, Michael took a trip to Germany to evaluate candle-making machinery. He returned with the notion to redesign his store and set out to replicate a magical Bavarian Christmas village.

Within three years after opening, the Deerfield store alone—with its new appeal and its ideal location for summer vacationers, fall foliage visitors, and Christmas shoppers—enjoyed sales of $1 million.

By 1998, through diligent hands-on management and perseverance, Michael's business grew to fifty Yankee Candle retail outlets around the country. It was then that he accepted an offer to sell the company. For $500 million.

And it all started with a two-dollar godwink. Someone expressed appreciation for his craft and bought the candle he had made for his mom. He was nurtured by encouragement from Uncle Kraemer, who believed in him when others didn't, and from a stranger, from the man who'd said, "Why don't you give your candle thing a try?"

Today Michael loves to share his entrepreneurial counsel with students, and he occasionally lectures at his hometown colleges and elsewhere.

"I've learned that if you're going to be a good manufacturer, you've got to be a good retailer. If you're going to be a good retailer, you need to be a good shopper," he says, explaining that studying the shopping skills of his customers has always helped him preserve his edge in business.

Michael also peppers his talks with motivational principles, passing along words of encouragement sown in him by others years ago. Through his inspiring stories of believing in your dream, striving for excellence, and working hard, he leaves his audiences a bit better prepared to meet every one of life's new challenges and opportunities.

Finding the Compass in You

In the final analysis, Michael Kittredge forged his new beginning in life—his successful career in business—by following attributes already hardwired into his internal makeup: his passion to create candles.

So how do *you* uncover the attributes and passions that point toward the career path you should most likely pursue? The best starting point is to take an inventory of your innate strengths and interests. Determine what you are good at. Make a list of the talents you possess and skills you have already mastered. Think about which tasks are easy for you to perform.

Go ahead. Get yourself a pad of paper and start writing down honest answers to the following questions:

- Is it a joy for you to talk with people? Does interacting with others come easily to you and leave you energized? If so, perhaps you should find a job in retail that would place you in frequent contact with the public. Or consider working in sales, where you'd probably talk to people every day, and the more orders you generate, the more money you can make.

- Is it easy for you to organize meetings, events, or parties? Those attributes could lead you into marketing, event planning, or management roles.
- Is problem solving something in your comfort zone? Career pursuits in nursing, teaching, or government agencies may be the right fit.

Perhaps you like to cook or you love cars. Or maybe you enjoy traveling, reading, or taking things apart and putting them back together again …. Each of these interests could be inner compasses pointing you toward a career that is just right for you.

That's what Carol discovered.…

Carol: Espresso with Love

Like many mothers whose children have left the nest, like many people whose life challenges (divorce … downsizing … financial disaster) have thrown them into terrible uncertainty, Carol McManus found herself drawn into a whirlpool of depression; she didn't know which way to turn or how to get out.

She ended up following what Richard N. Bolles

identified as the most successful route to her future, the route with an 8 percent success rate: a "life-changing job hunt."

What do you bake for the president of the United States?

Since arriving at her tiny coffee-and-pastry shop on Martha's Vineyard that morning, Carol McManus was unable to shake the question. After all, think what a visit by the president would do to catapult her fledgling business. It would bring her publicity, it would attract customers, and it would be fun!

Her shop, Espresso Love, occupied an odd-shaped corner of a hotel one block from Edgartown Harbor. The space had remained vacant—too petite and peculiar for most shopkeepers—until she opened for business one year earlier when her life took a 360-degree turn from the depths of anxiety and financial ruin.

Look at me now! What a difference a year makes, thought Carol. *Who would have thought a year ago that I could do this—start a business I knew nothing about…bake my own creations every day … serve customers who like my pastries … pay down a mortgage … and make bankruptcy payments!*

Then Carol's mind drifted back to one very desperate morning when she was still battling a yearlong bout of depression. She slid from her bed to her knees and pleaded with God: "Please take this sadness away from me. I'm so sad my marriage ended. I'm scared for my five children. I don't know how to make a living. I'm afraid to move on. Help me to find a way, Lord. Help me make a living using talents and gifts I already have. Please, please help me!"

Within a day or so, Carol's fervent prayer seemed to be answered: She had a godwink.

She was watching ABC's *20/20* program. It was 10:10 p.m. The reporter described a phenomenon occurring throughout the Northwest: Small, friendly coffee and cappuccino shops were opening up left and right. They sold baked goods and encouraged customers to hang out, read newspapers, go online, and socialize with friends.

"I could do that!" said Carol with wide-eyed enthusiasm. She loved baking. She loved interacting with people. What more would she need? Well … money, of course.

You just filed for bankruptcy, said an inner negative voice.

I know, I know, replied her positive side. *But I love serving people. That's one of my strengths!*

What do you know about running a business? derided the negative voice.

"I can learn!" Carol shouted out loud.

She instantly concluded that seeing the story so soon after her urgent prayer was more than coincidence: It was a godwink affirming her destiny.

A small ad in the Martha's Vineyard newspaper caught Carol's eye, and she promptly went to look at the space near the corner of Water Street and Main. Later, someone at the Edgartown National Bank, located across the street, stated that a "For Rent" sign had hung in the window for three years.

Carol's conviction to move forward with her idea was so strong that, on that Friday morning, she nervously wrote a check for $100 to hold the space—and she knew full well that the check couldn't be covered by funds until the following Monday. Then she set out on a journey of discovery, unveiling the unknown about starting a business: She hired a carpenter to build countertops and cabinets (when there was no money to pay for them right away); she learned which building permits were necessary; and she talked with some shopkeepers in the area to determine other factors essential to a successful enterprise.

"May I pay you in a month?" she would cheerfully ask everyone, with a sweet, innocent smile.

Several weeks later, Espresso Love opened. There was no sign yet hanging outside, and the only thing for sale was coffee and cake, but on her first day, Carol took in $250. And that ignited her confidence that she could really do it: She really could run a business.

Espresso Love had a comfortable cheeriness about it, a friendly, inviting ambience. As a statement of Carol's faith and reflection of her basic values, she placed a bowl of tiny cards next to the cash register, each containing a single word representing a biblical principle. Customers soon came to understand that pulling a card from the bowl provided them with one word's worth of fuel for the day: TRUST, LISTEN, SMILE, and so on.

"Business just kept growing during that first year," says Carol. "Then, the following summer, the entire island was buzzing with excitement: President Clinton chose Martha's Vineyard for his vacation. I started thinking, *What a great thing it would be if I could get him to come to my shop.*"

But island residents were divided in their opinions. Would the entourage of a vacationing president cause too much hassle—and too many traffic jams—for their small island?

Some citizens said yes, but most shop owners said no.

A woman entered Espresso Love and identified herself as a reporter from the *New York Times*.

"What do you think of the controversy over the president's visit?" she asked Carol.

"Oh, I think it's wonderful," she responded as an idea popped into her mind. "In fact … I'm … going to make a muffin for him. A presidential muffin."

"Really?" said the reporter, jotting a note on a pad.

As soon as the reporter departed, Carol started asking everyone who came in, "What do you think a presidential muffin would look like?"

She herself had absolutely no idea.

Determined to be prepared just in case the president of the United States did walk into her shop, she called the White House. Transferred to a succession of people, she eventually spoke with a chef on the kitchen staff.

"What kind of baked goods does the president like?"

"He likes everything" was the answer.

Not much help.

So Carol made a decision. A white cheesecake muffin decorated with blueberries and strawberries–that would be the presidential muffin.

Every day during President Clinton's two-week vacation on Martha's Vineyard, Carol rose early to do her baking at home. Then she would transport the baked goods to the shop in time to open at 6:30 a.m. Every day she made a batch of presidential muffins. Every day she set aside one muffin on a rack next to a sign that read: "Save for Bill." And every day the muffins sold out.

But the president never came in.

Two weeks of hullabaloo finally died down, all the reporters disappeared, and the Vineyard returned to normal. Yet there was one positive outcome for Carol. A story in the *New York Times* mentioned that a small coffee shop, Espresso Love, had made special red-white-and-blue presidential muffins in honor of the famous island guests.

The following summer the island began buzzing again about another presidential visit. A woman entered Carol's shop and identified herself as an associate of the White House.

"I've told the Clintons about you," said the woman who'd seen the *Times* article the previous year. "Could you put together two of everything every morning? I'll have someone pick it up."

For two weeks Carol was thrilled that her baked goods were being transported, presumably, to the President and First Lady. Yet, she was on pins and needles wondering if they liked them—and wondering whether her dream would come true. Would President and Mrs. Clinton actually visit Espresso Love? But Carol's hopes were waning.

By the end of the two-week frenzy over the presidential visit, not only were Carol's spirits sagging, but so was her energy.

"Why don't you just stay home this morning?" suggested Carol's son T. J. "You're exhausted. I'll open up myself."

"Okay," she sighed with relief.

But within the first hour of opening, an official-looking person came into Espresso Love and announced, "The presidential party is on its way. Please stay put. Make no phone calls."

T. J. panicked. *No phone calls?*

He had to tell his mother.

Secretly he went to a phone, hastily called Carol, and told her the exciting news. She dropped the phone and immediately flew out the door.

"I was running down the sidewalk," says Carol. "I was all out of breath, and the Secret Service spotted me, a woman running toward them. They got nervous!"

"I'm the owner!" she shouted.

Quickly wrapping herself in an apron and swiping some lipstick across her lips, Carol McManus was standing proudly behind the counter when the president, wearing a blue shirt and a red ball cap, came into her little coffee shop with the First Lady and others.

"I just wanted to meet the woman who was doing the baking for me," said the president with a smile on his face and a twinkle in his eye.

Carol smiled and shook his hand as T. J. snapped a picture.

Mrs. Clinton fished a card from the bowl near the cash register. Unaware of what her future would portend, she smiled as she read it: FORGIVENESS.

Perhaps instinctively Carol had known that the honor of a presidential visit to her shop would be a turning point for her business. And it surely was. After that day, many more people seemed to want to get their coffee and scones where the president had gotten his.

Carol's business surge was the good news. The bad news—from the landlord's point of view—was the line of people snaking in front of the hotel entrance and the crowds that were hanging out at the tiny shop. Carol received a jolting notice: Her lease would not be renewed.

"All things work together for good for those who love the Lord," Carol kept reminding herself, searching for the good that she was sure was going to come from this sudden adversity ... even though, for the life of her, she couldn't see it just then.

T. J. was working part-time at a restaurant behind the Dukes County Courthouse. Charlotte, the restaurant owner, was planning to move her business to a Main Street location.

"Why don't you ask your mother if she wants to buy this place?" Charlotte said to T .J. "The purchase price is $1,200,000."

"I couldn't afford that," said Carol when T. J. mentioned it to her. *"Or could I?!"*

She decided to investigate the requirements for taking on a mortgage of such proportions. She walked across the street to the Edgartown National Bank.

"I was way out of my league," says Carol, "but the bank manager was now a friend of mine and a good customer."

She explained her plight and the proposal to purchase the space behind the courthouse.

After patiently listening to her, the manager leaned forward and said, "We'll do anything to make the deal work, Carol. We've watched you build your business and witnessed your hard work, and we appreciate how you treat your customers. The Small Business Bureau loves supporting women who are growing businesses, so let's see what we can do."

Many people, however, warned Carol that she was indeed way out of her league.

"That's way too much debt," said some.

"You'll be leaving a perfect location on a main corner of town to go behind the courthouse where there's no walk-in traffic," argued many others. "People won't be able to find your shop."

The mortgage eventually went through, and on a dismal rainy day in late April, Carol officially opened Espresso Love in its new location. Most people wondered if Carol's business would even survive.

But every umbrella-toting supporter who turned out was instantly encouraged to see a long line of other umbrellas stretching all the way across the parking lot to the rear of the courthouse: Faithful customers were waiting in line to get into Espresso Love on opening day.

"I didn't even know I had this ability inside me," said Carol with self-effacing astonishment at her progress as a businesswoman. "I prayed that God would send the people to find me—and He did!"

Sitting over a cup of coffee with a friend and casting her eyes around at the charming and homey décor of her establishment, Carol shared a conviction: "When I bought Espresso Love, I was buying it for all women." And, to other women she meets who are seeking a new beginning in life, Carol counsels them to hold on to their dreams and to look for the signposts of reassurance.

Today Carol is also an author and speaker. In her colorful cookbook Tabletalk, she endorses the timeless principle that the sharing of food and family, during regular gatherings at the dinner table, promotes love.[3]

"Can you imagine my godwink? Right after my desperate prayer asking God what to do, I 'happen' to see a story about people opening up coffee shops … at 10:10 p.m. on 20/20. How perfect was that?!"

Chapter

7

PERSONAL REQUESTS

When we hear the term new beginnings, one of the first thoughts is usually career related. But many new chapters in life have nothing to do with jobs, and these beginnings are just as scary.

Marriage, for one. And I'll repeat what I've said in my other books: No couple should enter marriage without learning to pray together for at least five minutes a day. When you make praying together a priority, you'll understand why the Baylor University/Gallup research reported in *Couples Who Pray* shows potential for a 20- to 30- percent increase in romance, conversation, and happiness. Go to coupleswhopray.com to find out more.

Having a family is another new and quite extraordinary beginning. I've often asked first-time parents, "Did you have any idea that parenting would be like this?" With dazed, sleep-deprived eyes, they invariably shake their heads no.

Buying a new home for the first time is one of the scariest of all new beginnings in life. The total size of the transaction, often involving more money than most of us have ever seen, can trigger unexpected palpitations and anxieties. A jumble of what-ifs begins to scream inside your head: *What if I lose my job and can't pay for it? What if the house needs major repair and my savings account gets depleted? What if my neighbors turn out to be difficult people?*

If a real estate transaction is in your future, the next two stories may give you some solace….

Karen: Godwinks for a Panic Attack

Karen was feeling physically sick as she and her fiancé entered the financial adviser's office to sign papers.

"My heart was pounding, my skin felt tingly, I was sweaty, and I could barely think straight," she said. "I was starting to feel extremely scared, paranoid. It was the closest thing to a panic attack I had ever felt."

The pending wedding plans seemed easy by comparison to this, the biggest purchase of their lives.

Karen and Jordan had studiously looked at many options. They had decided the best value would be found in buying a new home in a development community. Getting in on the ground floor, so to speak. The financing offered by the developers was more suited to their budget, the model homes gave helpful decorating styles to draw from, and there would be a neighborhood of other young couples going through similar experiences.

Over several weeks Karen and Jordan had looked at several new home developments, balancing the benefits of one against the other, studying one floor plan after another, and taking into consideration their dreams for starting a family, having visitors stay with them, celebrating holidays, plus a myriad of other factors.

They were nearly exhausted from looking at scores of photographs in sales brochures. Then one day a particular development home captured their attention. It seemed to resonate above all others they had looked at. The floor plan was called "The Buxton."

"Upon seeing the house, we immediately looked at each other and said, 'This is it,'" remembers Karen. "We both fell in love with The Buxton and got the wheels in motion to make the purchase."

A verbal agreement with the developers soon led to the time for them to sign the papers.

"I could barely focus while our financial adviser explained the clauses," said Karen. "I started feeling scared. I asked God to give me a sign. I didn't know what kind of a sign I was looking for or when I would receive it. I just knew I needed something to calm me down, give me peace, and let me know that we were doing the right thing."

Even though she had never had a panic attack before, Karen started to feel she was about to experience her first. Her heart started beating faster, her palms grew sweaty, and she started to feel lightheaded. The fear of possibly losing control of herself added to the stress of the situation. Her eyes revealed the fear churning within her as the financial adviser carefully explained one line after another in the enormous packet of contract papers.

"I started saying a prayer, like a mantra in my head, and asked God to give me peace while I signed my life away."

The adviser reached to the floor, lifted up his large black briefcase, and placed it on the table directly across from Karen. Then her fiancé's eye caught something. On the zipper of the briefcase was a tiny strip of metal with a name on it.

"Oh!" her fiancé exclaimed. "Look at that!"

Karen turned to see what Jordan had noticed.

"Look at the name on that zipper," he said to her excitedly.

Karen blinked, looked at the financial adviser, and asked, "Do you know the name of the house we're buying?"

He shook his head.

"There, swinging on the zipper of the briefcase carrying the papers needed to buy our first home, was a tag with the word *Buxton*," Karen remembers.

"Afterward, whenever I felt anxiety about the house, the upcoming expenses, and whether we did the right thing, I would instantly think of my godwink moment and feel immediate peace."

At various points in her life, Karen had prayed and asked for signs, but she is still amazed to have received such obvious confirmation so soon after asking. The fact that God spoke to her so quickly and clearly provided comfort during the stressful days of moving to a new neighborhood.

Karen and Jordan are living happily ever after. Their new home is everything they'd hoped it would be. They have wonderful neighbors, their finances are in order, and they love going home to a feeling of peace, comfort, and divine order. Their godwink moment proved to be a confirmation that they are exactly where they belong.

Tim: McAbee of Mayberry

Tim McAbee earned quite a reputation as a concert promoter and producer of acclaimed stage performances in the Pigeon Forge, Tennessee, area—down the road from Dollywood—where families love to vacation in the foothills of the beautiful Great Smoky Mountains.

Over the course of several seasons, for instance, Tim delighted audiences with multiple stage reunions based upon his all-time favorite television series *The Andy Griffith Show*. He paid tribute to Mayberry, the fictional town on the show, by reuniting such original cast members as Don Knotts, who portrayed Deputy Barney Fife; Betty Lynn, who was Barney's girlfriend Thelma Lou; George Lindsey as Goober; and Howard Morris as Ernest T. Bass.

Tim's business had progressed so sufficiently that he, who was single and living in a rental apartment, started thinking about buying a home. One day at the gym, he expressed that thought to a woman walking on the treadmill next to his.

"I'm selling *my* house," she replied.

As the conversation continued, the woman asked about Tim's occupation. He explained that he often rented a particular theater in town and produced his own shows and concerts.

"I bet you know my next-door neighbor," she commented. "He performs in a production show at that theater. His name is Bubba."

"Yes. Bubba's a friend of mine," replied Tim excitedly. *Now that's a godwink,* thought Tim. It was a term he'd only recently heard about, and he had come to use it whenever those little divine things happened that others might call a coincidence.

Later, while driving home from the gym, he wondered if he should go and see the woman's house, but all sorts of questions crossed his mind. *Maybe it's too soon to make that big an investment. What if something happens to the economy and people stop attending shows?*

Two weeks later he was again at the gym running on the treadmill next to the same woman whose house had been for sale.

"Any luck in selling?" he asked, secretly hoping it might still be available.

"Oh, I sold it the day after it went on the market," she replied, filled with satisfaction.

All the way home Tim kept kicking himself about his hesitancy in making a home investment.

A year later he finally came to terms with his fear and uncertainties and decided to do something about it. He called a broker and spent several afternoons looking at various homes in the Pigeon Forge area.

His consistent response was, "This just doesn't seem like the house for me."

Looking out the car window on the way to his final showing of the day, Tim spotted a small sign in someone's front yard that said, "For Sale by Owner."

After saying his good-byes to the broker, he decided to drive back and take a quick a look at that house with the sign. A phone number on the sign prompted him to call the owner who invited him right in to see the house.

"I just put the sign up this week, and already there are several interested parties," said the woman of the house.

As Tim walked through the house, it felt *right*; it felt like *the one*. It felt exactly like the kind of house, in the very kind of neighborhood he had dreamed he would live in. "I'll think about it and get back to you," said Tim as he left.

Upon calling back a few days later, he again was pierced with the deep disappointment of hearing those words, "The house has been sold."

Oh, no! he thought.

"Stay in touch, though," cautioned the owner. "You never know if the buyer's financing will go through or not."

Tim couldn't get the house off his mind. For days he thought about it over and over again. He pictured himself living in it … driving into that driveway after work … and how he would have decorated it. The feelings were so pervasive that he called the owner and said, "I know the house has been sold, but could I come back and tour the house again just in case the sale doesn't go through?"

The owner agreed. And as Tim walked through the home for the second time, those positive feelings he'd had earlier were reaffirmed.

As he looked out the kitchen window, checking out other houses in the neighborhood, the owner asked about his job. When he explained his work, the woman pointed to the house next door.

"Perhaps you know my neighbor. He's a performer. His name is Bubba."

Another godwink.

Tim couldn't believe it. This was *the* house. The *very* house he had missed out on buying the year before. Now it was on the market again—and he was missing out on buying it again!

For the next several days, Tim was dejected. But the divine alignment of GPS … God's Positioning System … often comes into play when we least expect it.

A phone call ended his torment.

"The other buyers couldn't get financing. The house is back on the market," said the owner.

"Wahoo!"

As he drove out to see his prospective home, Tim was overjoyed. Then the demons of doubt began to play with his mind again, fostering distrust in his judgment. *Yeah, yeah, yea … . Your business is doing better, but what happens if the real estate market falls apart?*

Tim drove down the street of his possible new home. He spotted the house. It *looked* like home. It was beautiful. But he decided to keep going, to drive beyond his potential home-to-be and see what the other houses in the neighborhood were like. As he came to the top of a rise, he spotted a street sign that he'd never seen before. His eyes widened with amazement.

It said, "Mayberry Lane."

If ever there was a godwink of encouragement from above—God speaking directly to Tim and saying, "Hey kid, you're on the right track"—it was that street sign bearing the name of the setting for his all-time favorite TV series *The Andy Griffith Show.*

Out of Your Comfort Zone

New beginnings occur when you are standing on the threshold of something you've never done before, something you've always wanted to do but never had the time, the courage, or the gumption to do.

Hopefully it is not too late to seriously consider the quest you've always thought about. Maybe this is the time to move out of your comfort zone, to step out in faith, and to just do it. You just may find it's one of the most rewarding experiences of your life.

It was such a time for Cristina....

Cristina: The Quest and the Rose

Absentmindedly arranging the vase of long-stemmed roses, Cristina Ferrare glanced around her comfortable Los

Angeles home. A twinge of guilt passed over her. Here she was, enjoying the fruits of her blessed life as a television host, former supermodel, and wife of a successful television executive, and so many others suffered from a devastating tragedy in their lives. But she was just about to measure, firsthand, the reality that lay between her abundance and the suffering of those less fortunate—and, frankly, she was nervous.

She was about to embark on the most daring quest of her life.

"I spotted a tiny mention in the church bulletin," says Cristina. "Volunteers were needed to go to Louisiana to help with the clean-up after Hurricane Katrina. At first I waited for what I call the 'pull.' I literally feel this undeniable pull, stirring within me. When I feel it, I know it's the Holy Spirit nudging me to step outside of my comfort zone. I felt it. So, I volunteered."

She agreed to journey to an area near New Orleans along with a handful of mere acquaintances—women from her church, Bel Air Presbyterian—to help the families still reeling from the death and destruction caused by the hurricane.

Cristina gently cupped her hands around the red roses as her mind drifted to the legend of the nun who became known as Saint Theresa. As a child growing up in an Italian Catholic family, Cristina was fascinated by the story of this young nun who wanted to become a missionary, but because of an infection from tuberculosis, she died at the age of twenty-four. During her last months of life, however, she wrote beautiful poems expressing deep spiritual wisdom. And it was through the childlike message of these poems relating to roses, that she became known as "Little Flower." With a sigh, Cristina placed the vase on the side table and went upstairs to pack for her trip.

Cristina began the journey out of sync. She had mistakenly left one day sooner than the other women from the church did, so she was all on her own when she flew into Shreveport Airport. As the plane descended, she recalled watching the graphic images of the hurricane's devastation on the nightly news. Those images still gripped her heart and played over and over in her mind. It made her ask herself, *What can I possibly do to help?*

Now that she was committed beyond the point of no return, a torrent of other questions crossed her mind. *Where will I stay? How do we get around? Where do you go to the bathroom?* She had no idea.

"It was night, and the only lights working outside were the landing lights for the planes," she recalls. "The airport was empty with hardly any signs of life."

Nervously, Cristina gathered her luggage and went outside to find a cab. As she looked around, her new reality was starting to hit. This was a far cry from her comfortable surroundings in Los Angeles!

"I found one cab idling on a dimly lit corner and thought for sure I was going to die and never see my family again."

But the taxi driver turned out to be a sweet man. He skillfully swerved through the debris on the darkened roads, and they arrived at a building that was barely distinguishable.

"Please don't leave me," said Cristina, stepping from the cab. Her intent was to have him wait while she

129

checked to see if it was the right place. But he must have misunderstood—and he drove off.

"I stood and watched the taxi disappear down the road for as long as I could see its taillights," she says.

Cristina entered the structure. Three large men were sitting at a table talking to a group of volunteers who stood, gathered, in front of them.

"The biggest and most ornery-looking man was seated on a metal folding chair, his big dirty feet up on the table," Cristina remembers. "He pointed to the only bathroom door and quickly announced that it was off-limits to the volunteers. He said that we were to use the toilets outside and pointed to the exit door."

"In the morning you are to line up, wash, and brush your teeth, and you'll shower at the end of the day after work," he said sourly.

Cristina decided not to test his temperament by asking where the showers were.

She was led to a tent and handed a small penlight.

"I just climbed into my cot and was quickly swallowed up by its frame. I felt like a hot dog," she said. "When I moved, the cot made such creaking noises, I thought for sure I would wake up my neighbors. Whoever they were."

At 5:00 a.m. Cristina rose and surreptitiously stole into the church to use the only indoor bathroom before anyone discovered her.

"This was my plan: Get myself ready before the sun came up, so I could call the airport and make arrangements to go back home."

She'd already had enough.

But as the others in her group began to arrive, she began to have second thoughts. She decided to hold off on her departure. To stay just one day.

Cristina could not believe her eyes as the battered old bus bounced along on muddy, rutted roads taking the group—now including the other women from her church—to their missionary destination.

"For miles and miles, for as far as the eye could see, was total destruction. Trees had fallen on houses and cars. The trees had been uprooted and landed on rooftops with their roots exposed in gnarly, twisted messes."

It was worse than Cristina had imagined.

Where do you possibly begin? she wondered, squeezing back tears that pleaded to come out. *How can the six of us make a dent in this horrendousness…in the aftermath of the worst natural disaster in our country's history?*

The bus pulled into the site and stopped.

A foreman supervising recovery operations promptly greeted them and gave them their assignment.

"Strip this small house down to the frame," he instructed. "This place is toxic with mold. Everything goes."

Cristina's doubt-filled eyes surveyed the catastrophe. There were heaps of trash. Soggy plasterboard hung grotesquely from the framing. A battered refrigerator was strapped shut with duct tape—a warning of the gut-wrenching stench waiting to greet anyone who opened the door.

How can we possibly make a difference, God?

With the hopelessness of reducing the ocean spoon by spoon, Cristina and her colleagues pulled on masks and rubber gloves and began the filthy, arduous task of cleaning out the structure.

Where DO you go to the bathroom around here?

For hours the women pried, pulled, and piled plasterboard.

I'm dying for a drink of water.

Shoveling the remnants of Katrina's wrath was backbreaking. Cristina's hands hurt. Her shoulders ached. She and her cohorts labored and labored.

"After that first day, I decided to stay on. And I worked at the site every day for ten days. It took two ten-hour days to complete a house. That is, to clean out all the debris that had been sitting in fifteen feet of water for days. Everything was soggy and heavy. There was mold everywhere. The smell literally doubled you over."

The routine was the same for each house: Pull everything outside and pile it up on the lawn.

"There we could see remnants of people's lives. Clothes they wore, family pictures once displayed, toys children had played with—everything that represented a family's life."

Cristina froze when she came across an American flag. It was folded in a triangle and zipped shut in plastic.

"I just stared at it for a long time…and thought of the family who had coped with yet another tragedy in their lives."

Reverently, she lifted up the flag and placed it on a chair sitting on the porch.

"None of us wanted to throw it in the trash pile," she says.

For over a week and a half, Cristina and her colleagues met many wonderful people whose houses they cleaned. Interestingly, most of them didn't want to cross that imaginary psychological line and help remove anything from their own homes. They only wanted to talk.

"They wanted to talk, to share pictures, and to tell stories about things that were salvaged. And when someone wanted to talk, whoever was within earshot at the time would simply stop what they were doing, sit down, and listen. It was more important than cleaning up. The stories broke your heart. Stories of heroism, heartbreak, and courage."

Finally, the six women were finished with their assignment. Their last house had been swept bare and was now just a structure of two-by-fours.

Drooping from exhaustion, the six stood and proudly surveyed the scene.

Cristina watched the foreman inspect their work. Then his eyes narrowed as he shook his head slightly

"You've done a nice job here, but one bit of mold will contaminate the whole house," he said with a sigh.

He pointed the handle of a shovel up toward the ceiling and tapped the stained, once-white tiles.

"This has got to go," he announced, departing briskly as if to avoid any moans from the volunteers.

"Our hearts sank. We had thought our work was finally done," Cristina remembers.

But, clenching her teeth, Cristina grabbed the shovel and began banging on the ceiling.

"It exploded, and fell like large, soft pieces of snow," she says. "It felt like we were in one of those Christmas globes you shake and watch as the snow gently settles down."

Suddenly the women were waist deep in the kind of Styrofoam popcorn you use for packing boxes.

"For a moment we all squealed like little kids. We kicked and threw pretend snowballs."

Squinting through the remnants of falling debris, Cristina could see that her swept-clean floor was now a total mess. She and her friends were covered in white; the packing popcorn stuck to their clothes and hair.

Cristina sank to the floor.

"I suddenly felt angry, confused, disheartened, disillusioned, tired, and sore. I knew that picking up the debris from the floor was minuscule compared to the disastrous devastation outside—but it was suddenly so overwhelming.

"We had been there for ten days and it seemed that we had hardly made a dent," she agonized. "I felt we had made no difference at all."

With tears tracing paths in her dust-covered face, she simply could not believe this outcome. As every muscle in her body screamed, "Leave me alone!" her heart felt like it was going to break. She felt like vomiting. Instead, she just cried.

Another woman put an arm around her shoulder and comforted her, but it seemed hopeless. Totally hopeless.

As Cristina kneeled on the floor, she pleaded with God

for answers … for hope.

God, what are You doing here? What is this all about? Why so much heartache and destruction? Where is the hope? Where is the hope for these people, Father? Where is the hope?

Slowly she opened her squeezed-shut eyes. Her predicament came back into blurry view.

What's that?

Something seized her attention. Something red in the sea of whiteness.

She reached out and picked it up.

"It was a long-stemmed silk rose. It was in perfect condition and beautiful. It startled me because of the significance roses have in my life," she says.

Cristina gently held the flower in her hand and silently acknowledged that she was the beneficiary of a wonderful godwink.

"It was a definite sign. Christ was communicating to me as if I were a child again, when, in my innocence, I had faith, trust, and hope." She looked up.

Did the rose fall from the ceiling? Was it once hidden there by a member of the family who lived in this home?

Or, was this flower delivered on the wings of angels, directly from Saint Theresa, just as she had promised in her poetry?

This Cristina knew for certain: The tiny flower in her hand was a sign of life and hope.

"God was reassuring me that He is always there for us no matter how knee-deep in things we are—even if we're in over our heads."

When Cristina returned home to Los Angeles, she revisited the poem she'd once read as a schoolgirl, a poem written by the nun who lived only twenty-four years. To witness the devastation of Katrina against the backdrop of Cristina's own life journey, the poem became so much more meaningful to her.

The Flower
by Saint Theresa

All the earth with snow is covered,
Everywhere the white frosts reign;
Winter and his gloomy courtiers
Hold their court on earth again.
But for you has bloomed the Flower

Of the fields, Who comes to earth
From the fatherland of heaven,
Where eternal spring has birth.
Near the Rose of Christmas, Sister!
In the lowly grasses hide,
And be like the humble flowerets,
Of heaven's King the lowly bride!

Cristina's mind often returns to that day when she knelt on the floor of a small house near New Orleans; that day when her tear-covered countenance was transformed from sadness, to surprise, to joy. The long-stemmed red rose, like Saint Theresa's "Rose of Christmas," had lifted her up with the utter joy of hope.

"It was a godwink of hope directly from my Lord Jesus Christ—meant especially for me. Just me."

Cristina returned to the devastated areas of Katrina several times.

"I am so happy I went, and I will return again and again until I'm too old to go, because it will take years to rebuild. At least I know that when I face God, I can add this to my résumé … and He'll smile."

Chapter

8

CONCLUSION

This is what I hope you'll take away from this book:

- At the outset, I presented you with this promise: You can improve your perspective about where you want to go in life by following the lessons found in these incredible "life-altering stories about people just like you, who have stood on the threshold of new beginnings."

- I also suggested that, in much the same way that the people in this book did, you can develop the ability to resist both negative comments and the belittling of your dreams by girding yourself with perseverance, focusing on what you believe to be your destiny, and then heading toward it.

- You've seen in this book how each person was guided by signposts of encouragement that I call "godwinks." You'll find that these so-called coincidences and answered prayers in your own life will help you navigate your journey, and guide you to "destinations with quests fulfilled."

- As Lewis Carroll's Cheshire Cat taught us: If you don't know where you're going, any road will take you there. So you need to first establish where you want to go and then map a path to get there. And focus on that goal daily.

- Cheryl McKay and Tom Harken showed us that a strong belief in God leads to a stronger belief in yourself.

- Building a relationship with a friend is always based on your communication with that person; therefore, having a strong relationship with God begins with daily communication. With prayer. As Tom Harken's story showed us, God even hears the prayers of little kids.

- God also hears long-distance prayers. The story of Franklin Graham's praying parents demonstrated the effectiveness of prayers to our powerful God who rescued a powerless aircraft traveling through the night sky when both the plane and the nearest airport were dark.

- Hope is fueled by faith, and our faith is often boosted by the unexpected arrival of godwinks at just the right time—by an inexplicable number of monetary contributions for Yvonne to develop a school for disabled adults; by a series of odd license plates with messages of encouragement for Jeani; or by having a man Debbie had sought, for months on end, turn up in front of her at an obscure shop on the other side of the Atlantic.

- Help yourself! Don't sit by the side of the road on your baggage waiting for destiny to come to you. Step out in faith! Move forward. Head for what you believe to be your purpose in life. And, who knows. Perhaps, like me, someone will come along in a green Volkswagen to help you on your way.

- Words like *no* and instructions like "Give up!" belong in the basement of your priorities. As with Steven

Jobs, we need to meet rejection with reanalysis, repurposing, and sometimes even reinventing ourselves. As we learned from Vin DiBona, who demonstrated how to put the *ten* in *tenacity*, giving up should not be entertained, even after 136 turndowns.

- "If you do what you fear, you won't fear what you do," Gordon Morton told us.

- Richard Nelson Bolles advised that the Internet and newspaper want ads may be the worst place to find a job and that thoughtfully evaluating yourself, then calling on those who have the kind of jobs you want, has an 86 percent success rate.

- Michael Kittredge's story shows what can happen when you take an aptitude—in his case, making candles—and apply faith, persistence, and a refusal to compromise on quality.

- Carol McManus had hit bottom in her battle with depression when a godwink opened her eyes to a career pursuit that matched talents she already had: She loved working with people and baking. Putting them together resulted in a remarkably successful business.

• Karen, Tim, and Cristina revealed that when you are up to your eyebrows in the scariest decisions and quests in life, you are likely to find unexpected signposts of encouragement—delightful godwinks— that say, "Hey, kid! I'm thinking about you right now. Hang in there. You're on the right track."

Now that you've heard all these encouraging stories from people who have been in similar … or perhaps worse … situations as you, it's now up to you. Gather up confidence in yourself, ask God to be your guide, and then get going … head for what you believe to be your destiny!

Perhaps I'll meet you there!

Good wishes—and godwinks!
SQuire

ENDNOTES

Introduction

1. *Alice in Wonderland*, Lewis Carroll, Dial Press, 1931; pg 55; http://books.
   google.com/books?hl=en&id=HGIgGQYNpCsC&dq=Alice+Through+The+
   Looking+Glass+original+play&printsec=frontcover&source=web&ots=QAeW
   nqfOtr&sig=Qit61WWv_lBDBCUf5pUNVNMTcLc&sa=X&oi=book_result&r
   esnum=5&ct=result#PPR4,M1

Chapter 1

1. Tom Harken, *The Millionaire's Secret* (Nashville: Thomas Nelson, 1998); plus
   interviews with the author.

Chapter 2

1. Harold G. Koenig, David B. Larson, Michael E. McCullough, *Handbook of
   Religion and Health* (New York: Oxford University Press, 2001).
2. Wilbur Irwin, *Under His Wings* (Jackson, MS: *Baptist Record*, April 15, 1971),
   as reported by Franklin Graham in *Rebel with a Cause* (Nashville: Nelson,
   1995), 77, and anecdotally told to author by Dr. Joe McKeever, columnist,
   cartoonist, and former pastor.
3. Franklin Graham, *Rebel with a Cause* (Nashville: Nelson, 1995) 73–77.
4. Story fact-checked by Franklin Graham, August 2007.

Chapter 5

1. Zig Ziglar, *Ziglar on Selling* (Nashville, TN, Thomas Nelson Publishing, 1991)
   65–66.
2. Steve Jobs, *Commencement Address, June 12, 2005*, Stanford University.
   http://news-service.stanford.edu/news/2005/june15/jobs-061505.html.

Chapter 6

1. Richard Nelson Bolles, *What Color is Your Parachute* (Ten Speed Press,
   Berkeley, CA, 2009, pgs.32–36).
2. Richard Nelson Bolles, *What Color is Your Parachute* (Ten Speed Press,
   Berkeley, CA, 2009, pgs.32–36).
3. Carol McManus, *Tabletalk* (Edgartown, MA: Vineyard Stories, , 2008), xi.

COUPLES WHO PRAY by SQuire Rushnell and his wife Louise DuArt, is a groundbreaking book which dares partners to take The 40 Day Prayer Challenge™: Pray together five minutes a day for forty days. Nearly every couple reports life-changing results within days.

WHEN GOD WINKS AT YOU is SQuire Rushnell's third book in this word-of-mouth bestselling series. Do you sometimes feel alone? When godwinks come into your life, the author asserts that, out of six billion people on the planet, you are receiving person-to-person messages of reassurance from God.